ON ADULTING

How Millennials (And Any Human, Really) Can Worry Less, Live More, And Bend the Rules for Good

KATINA MOUNTANOS

SP

Skyhorse Publishing

10 9 8 7 6 5 4 3 2 1

Library of Congress Cataloging-in-Publication Data is available on file.

Cover design by Kai Texel

ISBN: 978-1-5107-5882-7
Ebook ISBN: 9978-1-5107-5883-4

Printed in the United States of America

To my parents, who always encouraged me to Reach for the Stars

To Dupi, who has the uncanny ability to see my dreams become reality before I can even imagine them

And...

To anyone who feels like their own dreams are impossible: the stuff that keeps tapping you on the shoulder won't stop until you listen.

CONTENTS

PREFACE

A Note to the Human Reading These Pages

Have you ever felt like you were *going through it?*

"Going through it" is a difficult feeling to describe in words. Urban Dictionary, ever the formal source, defines "going through it" as an experience that makes you soft and emotional. My definition is a bit more intricate (and a bit more realistic, if you ask me.) To me, "going through it" happens when everything around you seems to be falling apart. It's those moments in time when you watch your life as you knew it slip through your fingers like tiny grains of sand. From the outside you may look normal, but inside it feels like tectonic plates are beginning to wake up from a long hibernation. Many of us start "going through it"—whether we realize it or not—once we step into the "real world." We begin to see through all the B.S. we once believed, or maybe we just begin to see more clearly how distorted our vision was in the first place—and sometimes, all of that is too much to bear.

If you've ever gone through it (hey, maybe you are right now), you know that words, in any form, feel like a mirror to your soul.

They make you jolt up with excitement and wonder. It doesn't matter how you come across them. They could be in a book, or in a video, or heck, on a subway ad. But the moment that you feel seen, that your feelings are validated by some random stranger who felt the *same exact way*, you know that you're not alone. And, being not alone matters. It matters even more than the words themselves. Because when you're "going through it," every single breath takes effort. It feels like one small shift could send you crumbling. It seems like you're the only possible person in the whole entire world who could ever feel as crummy as you do right now.

So, when you realize that you're not alone—that these weird, confusing feelings are part of the shared human experience—a weight (or a crumb) falls away. You begin to look up, and maybe even take a peek around. You realize that this period in time when you're "going through it" is just that: a moment. And, that moment might teach you something.

Heck, it might teach others something. It might even shift the world for the better.

Oh boy, did I really go through it. A few years ago, when I entered The Club I Never Asked to Join—otherwise known as Adulthood—I was confused and sad and angry. It literally felt like my face was permanently scrawled into that *What The F*ck*-looking emoji (you know, the one with "&$!#%" coming out of its very red face.) Before I joined this club, I had a pretty run-of-the-mill life. One that most of you could probably relate to, because it was so . . . *normal*. Before that time, I had never really questioned my existential happiness. I mean, yeah, I had felt confused and sad and angry before—for big stuff, like when my grandma passed away before my dad could make it to see her in their tiny village in Greece, or little stuff, like when my high school soccer coach told me that I was probably better off running track instead (which, I most definitely was, though his observation still stung). But, it wasn't until I woke up every single day and realized that *this* was it, this was the life I worked so hard for that I started "going through it." And to me, it wasn't an experience that made me simply feel soft and emotional.

As soon as I could bear to lift my head up and observe all my fellow humans in this weird club, I couldn't believe my eyes. On one hand, it seemed like everyone else's days were going *so* well. They got on the subway and picked out their groceries every Sunday and did all that adult stuff we're required to without complaining, while I could barely keep one measly plant alive in my very small, very messy apartment. But, as I got closer and peeled back the layers a bit, I soon realized that this new reality was even worse than I thought. Because, for a while I thought that *I* was the one who was doing something wrong. I guessed that I just couldn't figure out this whole adulthood thing and soon I'd just have to suck it up, button that suit jacket, and fit in. But instead, I came to learn that all these so-called "good" adults were simply just taking the easy way out. They were settling for good *enough*. They were running from work to their kid's soccer games to scrambling to answer emails before bed, half-heartedly with one foot out the door. These people I once looked up to and wanted to be like were constantly in a process of negotiation instead of choice. And, even though I didn't know much, I knew one thing for sure: if *this* was going to be the rest of my life, something had to change.

Being the Type-A, over-achiever I was trained to be, I knew I needed to figure this all out. So, I began to do my research. I devoured words in all forms. I seemed to inhale books, attend workshops, and talk to as many people as I could about living a life that mattered to *me*, instead of the white man in a suit upstairs. One that was a *choice* rather than a negotiation. A life that didn't feel like I settled into the humdrum of Adulthood, only to wake up decades later and realize that it all passed me by. And in my most desperate moments, I made a promise to myself: if I ever figured "it" out, I would pay it forward. I would share my words and experiences with others who are "going through it" so they can begin to pick their heads up, too. So, they can see that they're not alone by any means, even if it feels like it. But most importantly, if I ever got this whole Adulthood thing under my belt, I wanted to make sure that none of us would ever have to settle for a life that wasn't our choice.

Yet the more I pulled back the layers—of both this weird world we were operating in and my own beliefs about them—I realized that I didn't need to wait until my version of Adulthood was perfect. I saw that this whole growing up thing was messy and confusing at every step anyway, so I might as well share my process of understanding it. And, the more that I stopped trying to fit this mold that I clearly wasn't meant to fit in, the less that I felt like I was *going through it*. Now, there are a lot of things that happened during that messy middle and trust me, the entire point of this book is to work through every single step of them. But for the moment, let's fast forward a bit.

There came a point in my young adulthood journey when I moved through the darkness of "going through it" and began to see the sprinklings of light as I figured "it" out. I managed to find a job that I liked better (much better) than the last, a person who I loved a lot (like, a lot a lot —Dupi, my then-boyfriend whom you'll hear about in this book—is now my literal dream fiancé), and a life that I was beginning to understand (let's just say I didn't need to buy new plants every week). It felt like this: you know the second that you finally get what it feels like to ride a bike without training wheels? Maybe your mom or dad lets go of you from behind for one second without you realizing, and as you're in motion, your little legs peddling hard and your mind going *crazy* with fear, you somehow steady yourself without falling. You're wobbly, yes, but you're not on the ground. And, any time you're not on the ground is a huge plus. Well, that's how this period of my life felt. I was finally, kind of, almost getting it.

During this messy-but-manageable time in my life, I knew that the only way to make sense of my shifting world was to write about it. Writing has always been my form of release, of understanding, of connection. But back in 2016, writing publicly without being a journalist was quite nascent. Blogging wasn't really a thing. Think about this: Medium, the publishing platform that now has sixty million active monthly users, was a tiny, underground writing site. Instagram was still a photo-collection app. And, the word "influencer" wasn't in our everyday vernacular. So, it was kind of odd for me to spend nights and weekends hacking away at crafting stories about my deep life experiences that literally no one would see. But I had a small, magical, invisible pull to share. And so, I started *On Adulting*, a tiny blog with two loyal readers: myself and my mom. I'm not joking at all. For a good amount of time I would send my deepest, darkest thoughts about life and the weird parts about growing up into the depths of the Internet, unsure if any human ever saw them other than us two. But each day, I would get a call from my mom that she "really loved" my story about having a panic attack on the subway before work. You know, casual stuff.

Nevertheless, even though no one was seeing my words, those words kept flowing. Those words poured out of me with so much heart that I knew one day they would reach someone, somewhere and help them lift their head up, too. And well, a couple of thousand humans picked their heads up. Over three years, On Adulting became a notebook-turned-blog-turned-community that reaches tens of thousands of people around the globe every single day. I went from scribbling away in coffee shops, or stealing time to write at my desk—to turning this passion of mine into a job. A real job. A job that impacts thousands of humans a day through storytelling and mindset-shifting and connecting. My purpose is to make sure that we all know, especially when we're "going through it" that we're never, ever alone. And most importantly, that the point of life isn't to collect as many trophies as possible while continuing to search for that ever-elusive feeling of "happiness" but instead, to feel fully *alive*, dammit. It's to stop running on that work-gym-sleep hamster wheel, and shift our worlds, or more like The World for good.

And now, these words are reaching you. Words really have the power to change the world, don't you think?

I can't wait to share these words and stories and lessons with you for the rest of our time together. If you couldn't tell already, this book isn't one of your typical "self-help" types of reads. It's a compilation of research, analysis, expert-approved tips, and even exercises that I've worked on with hundreds of Millennials in practice to change their lives (truly). It's also a real, deep look into the messy, weird, confusing journey that I personally went through to go from a life that I dreaded being part of to a life that was completely and utterly my choice. A life that was joyful and meaningful and fulfilling at the same time. A life that bends the rules for good.

Before we dive into all of that good stuff, you should know that this book was written in large part during a completely different time in our world's history. Even though that time was just a few months ago, it was one when our biggest worry was how fulfilled we felt in our jobs or if going out for another night of happy hour instead of meal-prepping in your tiny apartment kitchen meant that you were a bad person. (I'm being facetious, but you catch my drift.) Before 2020, we were living through a period of time in the world that was on a scale of hunter-gatherers to Uber Eats, pretty damn good. But, since then, a lot of us Millennials and otherwise have faced a reckoning: What's the point of it all? Does my existential happiness really *matter* if I can't pay rent? Or my parents die? Or my country continues to dwindle away? It seems like our world is on fire, and to say the least, we're all "going through it."

As I received my book from my editor, the very book I wrote to help inspire a generation (and a world) to live a life full of meaning and connection and choice, I wondered if these messages even mattered anymore. If the *adulting* struggles in the way we've talked about them for years, like which credit card to get or what city to live in, was relevant anymore. But, as I took some space to reflect, I realized that we need these messages more than ever. It's about damn time that we all stopped pretending we were robots, and finally listened to that voice that's been whispering in your ear for years. There's no reason to play in the safe lane anymore. You can think of me, this book, these words as a conduit for whatever you're going through right now—and whatever ideas you've been putting off for a "better" time. 'Cause, the only time is now.

So, as we "go through it" together for the duration of this book, remember this: wherever you are in this big Earth right now (maybe you're reading in between sobs in the bathroom, or maybe you're laying on your couch pretending email was never invented), these words found you for a reason. And, if you take anything away from them, know that no matter how confused or sad or angry we are on this journey toward Growing Up, no matter how much we feel like throwing our hands to the wind, we never, ever, ***ever*** need to settle for a life that's good *enough.*

We have the power to choose.

—Katina

INTRODUCTION

Adulting: Trust Me, It's Scary + Confusing + Weird for Everyone

What do you want to be when you Grow Up?

You've probably heard this question hundreds if not thousands of times in your life. I'm not sure when it shifts from an exciting, mystical question with endless possibilities to one that's anxiety-inducing and laced with judgment. One moment, you're playing with Legos, shouting out unrealistic answers from the top of your make-believe castle: "Astronaut! Chef! President!" And the next, you're trying not to hide your fear while muttering, "I'm not exactly sure, but I'm studying . . ."

In my case, I grew up in a family of immigrants and small-business owners, so like any good, first-generation kid I knew the "right" answers to that million-dollar question from an early age. Even then, I realized how important this question was to Adults. From my vantage point, it seemed like your entire life began once you Grew Up—and everything boiled down to getting that answer correct. I quickly learned how to score points with any adult in the room: grow up and *be* something—Corporate lawyer. CEO of a pharmaceutical company. Definitely *not* a writer.

Even as I got a little older, I held this question close to my chest. I loved seeing the reactions of complete strangers when, at the age of eleven, I told them that I wanted to become an Emergency Room Doctor (inspired by *Grey's Anatomy*, of course). Their responses were always the same: "Wow, you've got a smart one on your hands!" as they would wink at my parents. Or sometimes, they would get down to my eye level and make sure I understood the importance of my statement: "Get ready to make loads of money, little lady!"

Whenever these interactions would occur, I could feel my parents ooze with pride. I became so addicted to the feeling of earning praise, I continued to up the ante. I applied this high-achieving, validation-seeking mindset to everything I did, from the grades I earned in school (classic nerd move—I once broke down in tears when I got a ninety-freakin-two on a science test), to the clubs that I decided to join (academic team *and* lacrosse during the same season).

The scariest and simultaneously saddest part in all of this? I wasn't alone. All of my peers seemed to have figured out the "right" answers, too. The safe answers. The answers adults *wanted* to hear.

But it wasn't until years later when I finally turned those adult-approved answers into my own everyday reality that I realized it was all a trick. That everything I had been promised upon entering this fabled land—Adulthood—was a figment of my imagination. I thought that if I just followed the rules, if I just kept working really, really hard to score all the "right" answers I would happily glide into the rest of my life.

But, following that path had left me on the doorstep of Adulthood as confused and lonely as ever. Spoiler alert: I didn't end up becoming that Emergency Room Doctor as I had imagined all those years ago. (*Grey's Anatomy* did make it seem really fun, though if I'm being honest, they did not once mention what it took to pass Organic Chemistry.) But I did end up on another "right" career path. Months before college graduation, I accepted a seemingly "Very Important Job" according to all those adults at a large investment bank in New York City. By anyone else's standards, this was a good choice. It was an Adult choice. It was a choice that would make everyone proud when I said it out loud.

I couldn't put my finger on why, but for some reason as the months inched closer to my starting date I became more and more anxious. And, it wasn't just because I was about to start the rest of my life. I went to New York University, so I understood what it meant to live among the hustle. No, this change was subtler. Without consciously realizing it, I was slowly becoming skeptical of the Adults in the room, and what their lives *actually* looked like instead of watching them with kid-like innocence.

There was one day in particular, a rainy, spring evening when it all became clear to me. I was only about two months away from becoming a *real* adult and the world seemed to be opening up in a way that looked different than before. As I meandered down the New York City streets, completely unaware of how lucky I was to simply stroll without a destination, the sky turned grey and a late spring thunderstorm took hold. I ran into the corner supermarket with a rush of people, most of whom looked like they just left work or a funeral. They were somber and rushed—a sea of dark suits huffing and puffing as they uncomfortably navigated around each other without looking up from their phones. Some of them huddled by the door, waiting for the rain to pass. Others used this time as efficiently as possible, grabbing items off the shelves with a fervor I couldn't understand. I looked in my backpack and realized I had 25 cents (literally), the perfect amount for a slightly bruised banana, I thought. I broke off the best-looking one and made my way to the checkout line.

The lines grew longer as the rain pounded harder outside. I didn't yet know what it felt like to be constantly absorbed in email monitoring, so I took the time to observe my fellow grocery shoppers as we inched closer to the checkout counter. Every single one of them looked stressed out. Strained. Like the weight of the world was on their shoulders. I almost couldn't believe my eyes. It didn't matter if they were wearing a full suit or a sweatshirt with baby throw up on it—they appeared robotic. It was as if this moment was just one more breath, they had to take on their hundred-foot-long checklist, and there was no end in sight.

This realization almost made me want to vomit. I looked around in a state of near-panic, full well knowing that I was about to enter this strained, stressed-out world in a few short months. These people represented the Future Me, and it scared the shit out of me. I looked at myself and I looked at them, all of them, so different in their appearance but similar in their demeanor. I think I may have pinched myself to make sure I wasn't living in some weird, zombie apocalypse.

When I was sure that this was real life, the very life I created for myself by doing all the "right" things, I made a promise to myself then and there on the supermarket line for one measly banana during Thursday evening rush hour: I would never become one of *those* people. I wouldn't allow myself—or anyone else for that matter—to resign themselves to this type of life where a random Thursday afternoon felt enraging and tedious at the same time.

I never wanted to lead a life that took the living out of your eyes and glued them to your phone.

But that promise was easy to make (and keep) before Adulthood began. It was much easier to look at the work-gym-sleep hamster wheel from the outside in, and exclaim you would *never* get stuck running in loops. That you would never become one of *those* people.

. . . Until you do.

Until you find yourself too weary to brush your teeth before bed, let alone keep your plants alive. Until it feels like you can no longer recognize what true excitement feels like, because you're constantly pretending to cheer for Joe from Accounting's tenth email. Until it feels like you're so far away from the person you *thought* you would be you don't even remember her. Until you realize you're "going through it" for real.

It took me only a few weeks into my big-girl job to get to that place of complete desperation. I found myself rolling my eyes at supermarket clerks for taking one measly moment to laugh with a co-worker (who laughs anymore?), or *running*, more like sprinting, to the office printer to prepare my boss for what felt like daily "fire drill" meetings. I was so caught up on that hamster wheel that I didn't even realize how quickly it had happened. One moment, I was meandering in the rain and searching for a quarter to buy a bruised banana, the next I was sprinting to the subway at five-thirty in the morning, chugging coffee to fuel my brain. It seemed like I couldn't even remember that girl who questioned this life from the outside; she now seemed too naïve, too young, too far away from understanding what the Real World was like. But it only took one outwardly normal experience to look myself in the eye—honestly—and ask: is this the type of person you want to be . . . forever?

Fast forward a few months from the supermarket incident. It was early September, and we were still in the thickness of summer. Imagine the humidity that seemed to fill every empty pocket of air making the crowded, downtown New York City streets feel even more claustrophobic than they already are. As I charged out of my office at the end of a predictably dreary Wednesday, I couldn't help but tug at the awkwardness of my new uniform. I wasn't used to wearing anything other than sweatpants for long stretches of time yet, so this stuffy black suit still felt too big, too formal, too *adult* for me. Quickly though, my eyes darted from my own dark uniform to the sea of others, and I found myself lost in the hurriedness of New York's post-work commuter mania.

I finally made it through the crowds of robots to my subway stop. When I took a breath, I seemed to be carrying the weight of the world (or more like my entire apartment) on my shoulders. My work bag, gym bag, and lunch bag collapsed onto the floor while I waited impatiently for a semi-empty train to pass.

And then, I saw it. A tiny corner seat caught my eye as the subway train blurred past. I *needed* that seat, my brain screamed. In that moment I felt as if there was no other person on that subway platform who had a more terrible, dreary, boring, *normal* day than I did. I was, in fact, sitting down for more than twelve hours a day, but it felt as if I had run a marathon. If I read one more email from Joe in Accounting I was going to cry—I was sure of it.

So, when the subway doors opened I fought tooth and nail to get that seat. And, win that sweet relief I did. I sat down in a huff—work bag, gym bag, and lunch bag falling in a heap around me—taking up as much space as I thought I deserved after a no good, very hard adult day at work. But, as soon as I closed my eyes to relax for just a moment I felt a nudge along my side. My eyes snapped open to find a woman, immersed in conversation with a friend, squeeze her bottom in a barely-there seat next to me.

I immediately felt her sweaty body squish against mine, and although I too had sweat dripping down my temples there was a different heat that began to rise in my chest. A heat I couldn't control. A heat I had never fully experienced before. In this seemingly mundane moment, a wave of anger so deep washed over me that I was paralyzed with feeling. This anger rose through my body so quickly, so intensely that it caught me by surprise. While my mind was racing through all the reasons why it felt like this woman was wrong, I knew that there was a deeper reason for my anger. I wasn't angry at this woman. I was angry and frustrated—and quite honestly shocked at myself. I couldn't believe how quickly this whole adulthood thing turned me into a shell of a human, one that sprinted from Point A to Point F and got angry at anyone who stood in her way.

It was in that moment that I realized I was "going through it." So, after weeks and months of suffering all alone I began talking to my family, co-workers, and random strangers about how weird and confusing adulthood was. I just couldn't believe, or maybe accept, that no one else in the world felt that same anger as me. And, that no one else was angry at their anger, either. I was surprised, though, that simply sharing out loud how weird and confusing this journey was opened up space for me to begin to notice some beautiful moments, too. But, even when I slowed down enough to let that heat in my chest dissipate a bit, I would suddenly remember that I had no idea what the hell I was doing—and it felt like I would never figure "it" out.

I assume that's why you found yourself here, reading this book on Adulting and growing up. You might feel alone and lost and like you're "going through it" in some way, shape, or form.

Maybe one day, a few months into this weird, confusing journey you realized that you were *not happy*. Maybe years later, the curtain fell down. Maybe decades in, you are finally waking up to the potential that your life can hold.

Listen—I feel you. I was/am/probably always will be with you. But, after that seemingly mundane little subway incident, I decided to do something different. I began to wake the heck up. I slowly became aware of The Rules. I started to convince myself to take one tiny step off The Path. I stopped trying to collect all the "right" answers. Instead, I looked inside and figured out what made me light up. I saw that I could do the stuff that made me happy and fulfilled while also paying bills. I worked hard to understand all the layers I had built up over the years that clouded my vision and made me feel like a different person that I was deep down inside. I scrubbed and analyzed and cleared out whatever I could so that I felt like I was actually living—not merely existing.

Most importantly, I realized that it's also my *job*, my purpose on this big Earth, to show everyone out there that Adulthood doesn't need to be a never-ending To-Do list. That you could step off the work-gym-sleep hamster wheel, stand still for a moment, and your bills (or loans, or whatever) will still get paid on time. And heck, bills and promotions and five-year-plans aren't the *only* things we're living for, anyway.

So, let's dive into this weird, confusing, beautiful journey together. This book is going to be a mix of understanding, connecting, and reflecting. Like I told you, this isn't your typical "self-help" book. We're going to analyze everything from large-scale societal research to our own belief systems. We're going to vent like we're having a late-night wine session together and dream in our journal about our most perfect life without letting any barriers hold us down. We're going to systematically work through all the rules we've been taught to follow and figure out how to break them. We're going to figure out this whole Adulthood thing one simple step at a time.

We will start by laying all the rules on the table of this exclusive club we're all inducted into without a choice the moment that we enter our twenties. Then, we'll decipher advice from experts and scientists about *how* we became the little rule-following humans we are today both from a neuroscience and societal perspective. We'll enter Dream Land and answer those big life questions together (What am I doing with my life? What am I even passionate about? How do I actually do "adult" stuff like paying loans and making new friends and moving to new cities without drowning in self-doubt?). Finally, we'll make sure that this whole new mindset you're about to apply to your life is *sustainable*, and that it's something that you can continue to grow into well after you put this book down.

Sound like a plan?

Well then, take a deep breath and let's get started. I can't wait to begin this weird, confusing, beautiful journey—together.

Part One:

Welcome to The Club

Growing up is losing some illusions in order to acquire others.

-Virginia Woolf

What you are seeing and hearing right now is nothing but a dream.

-Don Miguel Ruiz

ONE

Things Are Not Always What They Seem

Remember when we were kids, and the summer carnival would come to town?

I grew up in a middle-class enclave of Long Island in the 1990s, one that felt squarely suburban. It was a place where all my friends' parents, except my own, were born within a ten-mile radius of our beachside neighborhood. You know, it was the type of American town where everyone knew everyone, and a time when AOL dial-up still consumed our phone lines. So, summer carnivals were *kind* of a big deal.

I remember those days fondly and, oddly, clearer than you may expect. The afternoons leading up to summer were muggy and humid to the point where you couldn't tell if the stickiness on your hands was from Fruit Rollup residue or sheer sweat. And, the carnival pulled into town on the precipice of those long, summer days. They set up shop in our train station's parking lot during the same weekend in early June each year, almost as a celebration for the season we were about to enter: one filled with Kool-Aid for lunch and afternoons spent running through the Crazy Daisy sprinkler then chasing down the ice-cream truck, barefoot, for a Cherry Screwball (you know, the one with the gumball at the bottom?). You remember them, the days when our biggest worry was if our Tamagotchi pooped while we were riding our Razor scooter around town.

Each year, I went to the summer carnival with a *crew*. My Manhunt sidekicks and fellow firefly catchers would make our way to the dressed-up parking lot by foot, what felt like miles ahead of our parents lagging behind with strollers (and maybe a Corona disguised in an unassuming red cup). But, while the other kids would line up for extra chances to win a goldfish or a candied apple, I would often escape the crowds finding myself in the Fun House with a handful of my less adventurous friends. We would walk around in there for what felt like hours, stealing glimpses of our odd figures in the distorted mirrors in front of us. It was almost as engrossing as a late-night Nintendo session—I couldn't peel my eyes away. I tried to act cool and normal, but inside I was freaking the heck out. If I would stop to stare back at my weirdly-long chin or bulging eyes for a moment too long, a shrill of nervous laughter would escape me. It felt like if I kept looking at this bizarre version of myself, I'd get stuck that way forever.

But, you know what the worst part of it all was? I felt like I *had* to play it cool. Even thought I was scared shitless, I pretended that everything was normal. And, I was oddly obsessed with the sheer uncertainty of it all.

If you don't remember the good ol' carnival days (maybe the Tilt-N-Hurl will ring a bell?) just think about how addicting it is to scroll through the warped, Instagram-filtered versions of your face. You know deep down you're the same person, but damn, staring straight back at yourself-as-your-dad can get creepy. Well, adulthood is kind of like you're stuck looking at yourself in a never-ending Fun House mirror—unsure of who you are at every twist and turn; worried that a monster (or long-lost childhood friend you haven't spoken to in years but keep up with on Facebook) might pop out of nowhere to throw you off your game.

On the outside, though, you act like everything is going swimmingly. Since it all seems oddly familiar, it feels weird to acknowledge the scariness. It's almost like you're walking around your kid bedroom in the dark: you think you know where everything is until you stub your toe on a forgotten T-Ball trophy and stifle an "Oh shit!" scream so your parents don't hear you curse. Unlike Fun Houses or Instagram filters though, the trick mirrors in Adulthood seem to literally appear out of nowhere. That's the craziest part. Because, it's not like entering Adulthood was a surprise to any of us. When you think about it, we've been preparing to get into this club for our entire lives. Everything we've done—from how we spent our free time as kids to the friends we made (and quite honestly, kept) were all for *this*. Every weekend-long dance recital to add to our résumé. Every TV show not watched in favor of SAT preparation. Every time your parents banned AIM chats because of a "bad" grade. Didn't they tell us the equation for success in adulthood was simple? Work hard in school, go to college, enter adulthood. From there, you're sure to have it made.

Just like at the carnival, from the outside looking in you can't tell that the mirrors are warped until you stare straight into them. Adulthood seems like a *dream* in our perfectly-curated world. Before you get here, it's portrayed as this place where you have the *freedom* to do what you want (summer excursions to unnamed European islands? I'll take it!), *money* to pay for stuff you care about (let's just say first dates are no longer at the town park), and *access* to cool stuff you weren't allowed to do before (enter trendy cocktail bars without a care in the world! pay for a rental car without $300 in extra charges!).

But, it's tricky. When you arrive in this fabled land where five dollars can now supposedly get you one fancy Matcha latte instead of dinner for an entire week, there's an immense pressure to get "it" right almost immediately. To have it all figured out from the moment you step off that graduation stage and into this exclusive club you never even asked to join. You're expected to handle your life like everything is perfect, even though you can't stop staring at your deformed face in the mirror. And, if your experience was anything like mine, you may have felt personally victimized by Adulthood from the moment you got here. You realize, almost immediately, that this dreamworld that adults brag about is a façade for stuff like bill-paying and HR deadlines and healthcare enrollment. It's like you were somehow dropped into an alternate universe with no instruction manual and a lifetime subscription to Bravo shows as the soundtrack to your now very boring life. This wasn't close to the Carrie Bradshaw-inspired daydreams you'd been cooking up instead of paying attention during your senior year accounting class.

The worst part of it all is that everyone acts like this whole schtick is normal, even though they can see the trick mirrors, too. And for some reason, you're supposed to just *accept it*. That even though you worked so hard to get *here*, a place where you are supposed to be *happy*, nothing is as it seems. You're suddenly living in a world where your life is defined by how you spend your two-week vacation (if you're lucky) and the name of the gym you pay to barely make an appearance at each month. And then, right before your eyes, one year has passed (then five! then ten!) and you still feel exactly the same. But, here's the trick: now you're the one that everyone looks to as the *adult* in the room, even though you couldn't feel more alone and scared and confused inside.

Adulthood has a lot of baggage. Unsuspecting, not-talked-about, secret baggage. It's like your life turned into a never-ending maze around the Fun House: everything looks weird and confusing, but oddly normal, too. So, we're going to break the first rule of this exclusive club and *actually* talk about all this stuff everyone tries to brush under the rug. Because, before we can fix any of it, we have to understand what we're fixing. We have to understand why these trick mirrors appeared in the first place. We have to all get on the same page, so at the very least, we're not confused about what we need to make better.

As we dive into this book, trust me, we're going to come up with a lot of solutions. We're going to do a lot of reflecting and thinking and planning to create the life that you badly want to live right now. But for the moment, let's think about this chapter as a glorified vent session. We're going to air it all out—feel *all* our feelings—and shine light on all the Fun House mirrors that appear once we enter Adulthood. All the confusing parts that no one likes to talk about. The stuff that never comes up at the water cooler or at happy hour with friends. Because, the first step toward healing anything—toward crafting this life that you so desperately want, instead of one you want to escape from—is being honest.

Trust me, when I first got here I was confused AF. I mean, you remember how my face looked, right (hint: *What-the-F%$#$-looking emoji*)? We're going to dive into the science behind why it's important to be honest about our feelings in order to make change later during our time together, but simply drawing from my own personal experience, when I finally started being real about what was so difficult, and what I was really feeling, I opened space for change. So, let's start by getting real about the shit everyone pretends is normal when you get into this really fun, cool new club you never asked to join.

Fun House Mirror Number 1: It's supposed to be cool, normal, and easy, they say

When I first joined this club, my naivety showed a lot. Like, it *really* showed. I didn't get why everyone was so intent on pretending everything was cool, normal, and easy when it felt exactly the opposite. I was confused why no one was talking about how difficult it was to navigate this new world. I knew, personally, that I didn't feel good right now. I also kind of knew that my darkness probably wouldn't last forever. But, you know what worried me the most, more than feeling lost or confused? That I felt entirely alone. That it seemed like I was the only human being in the world who had ever arrived on the doorstep of this club and was surprised by how much it sucked. I felt like I had to put on this fake smile dripping with happiness in front of my co-workers, roommate, friends, and sometimes even my family. I had to pretend everything was fine, even though I was crumbling inside. And, since it *seems* so normal from the outside, you feel guilty complaining about it. You feel like you're supposed to just "suck it up" because this is "what Adulthood is." You don't want to be cast as just another lazy, entitled Millennial who hates their job and depletes their non-existent savings on $14 Sweetgreen salads every day at lunch.

So, you work really, really hard at hiding your disappointment. You feign excitement when yet another team bonding session gets added to your already-packed schedule. You churn through emails and master PowerPoint slide decks and become extremely efficient at food shopping. All the while, you can't help but feel an emptiness that keeps on growing somewhere deep inside of you. You can't figure out why. Isn't this *supposed* to feel different? Better? Happier? Soon, you fear, that that feeling will grow so big you can't hide it any longer.

These types of things aren't casual conversations to bring up say, with your roommate, or your boss at work. How do you begin to have a chat about the fact that Adulthood is a blatant lie? That everything you had been taught somehow just doesn't add up? I know in my case, I channeled my confusion about what I was feeling on the inside into making sure my life on the outside looked the complete opposite. I did just as all the adults in the room were doing. I made sure to keep "raising my hand" at work. I signed up for stuff I'd never done before, like volunteer programs and running marathons (literally) and put extravagant vacations on my newly-minted credit card. I went from shopping at my neighborhood bodega for twenty-five cent bananas to Whole Foods, and felt the pressure to share all of it with my "friends" on social media.

Instead of being real about what I was feeling, I pretended that everything was just fine.

Until one day, it grew so big I couldn't hide it any longer.

Now, our world today doesn't make it *easy* to talk about our feelings. So, most of us keep trudging along with this silent pit of unhappiness and unfulfillment deep in our core. And, it's not just us Millennials either. According to The Harris Poll, a survey that's been measuring happiness for over a decade, less than a third of Americans consider themselves *happy*. Over 50 percent of working Americans feel like they're running on the work-gym-sleep hamster wheel with no end in sight. More than 75 percent of people *around the world* feel like they aren't living up to their creative potential, and don't have the "time" to do stuff that makes them feel alive.

And likely, because our culture today is so centered on productivity and busy-ness especially as we enter adulthood, we as a society are lonelier and less connected than ever. Literally—over

70 percent of adults today say that they only have one close friend. One! But you'd never guess from our social media profiles, and heck, that's definitely not counting our thousands of Facebook "friends"—you know, ones that we share our highest of highs with. Our reality in our modern world is continuously shaped by other people's wins—their engagements and children's first words, and their new job in London. I mean, it's all we see. Over 60 percent of us begin scrolling through social media and emails within 5 minutes of waking up, so we're already stuck in comparison mode before our first sip of coffee.

It's a continuous cycle for us Adults in our world where it feels like our worthiness lies in who our LinkedIn bio says that we are. It's like we're robots in The Sims—everyone feels unfulfilled, unhappy, and unsure of what to do next, but we walk around stone-faced and perfect. And then, we think there's something wrong with *us*, because we can't even seem to figure out how to fold our sheets while Sally is out there living her best life as a yoga teacher in Bali.

I mean come on, we all know a Sally, don't we?

Well, I'll never forget when I came face-to-face with my first real-life Sally. It was the first time I saw a tiny crack forming in my reflection as I stared back at myself in Adulthood's distorted mirror. I had been keeping my brave face on for what felt like *forever*, acting like I was obsessed with my job (even though I despised going into work every day), my apartment (a tiny fourth-floor walkup), and my social life (let's just say I barely remembered what happened past Friday at 5pm) to anyone I knew. So, when an old college acquaintance asked to catch up over a drink after work one day, I didn't think much of it. This girl, we'll call her Sally, seemed like she had it made from what I saw of her life on Instagram: a job at a really cool startup, travel plans that took her around the world, and constant invites to New York's trendiest clubs. At the very least, I definitely didn't head into that catch-up ready to bare my soul to her.

But, Sally did. To this day, I'm still not sure why she chose me of all people as the one with whom she would share her deepest struggles. We didn't know each other that well in school, but after two glasses of wine, I knew how difficult this transition into adulthood had been for her. And oddly enough, it sounded almost exactly the same as what I was feeling. That night we confided in each other, and now bound by our shared struggles, I walked into the cold December evening feeling a tiny glow lit within me. Maybe it was the wine—but likely, it was knowing that one person, one human being felt *the same exact way* as I did. And, it gave me the courage to be a little more honest. A little more open. A tiny bit more vulnerable to the struggles, because I didn't feel the immense need to be perfect any longer. And, I knew that if one person could be brave enough to share their struggles, maybe there are others who needed to see that light first before they could parse through their own.

Fun House Mirror Number 2: The Path is completely black and white, they say

I've done a lot of thinking, and reflecting, and researching *why* the transition to Adulthood (or any big, life transition for that matter) can be so weird and confusing in our culture today. And, I'm going to be a bit brutal here, but here's the honest answer: we've never been taught to think for ourselves.

Up until this point, we've lived a life of checklists and To Do's. We were trained to follow The Rules. We lived in a completely black-and-white world. We all sought out the "right" answers—the ones that made adults in the room ooze with pride. We were taught to become little robots who followed the equation: work hard, go to college, get married, buy a house, have kids, retire, take a cruise to Alaska (if you're lucky). We've all been shown the possibilities of meritocracy at every stage we've passed. Each checkpoint we made it through was like getting 100 gold stars in Mario Kart. We've been told thousands of times in thousands of different ways: stay on The Path, and you'll be rewarded with "success." The only issue is that no one ever took the time to explain what "success" really meant.

Or better yet, no one had us define it for ourselves.

Think about this for a moment: I bet you could still recite the rules for how to write a DBQ essay or remember how to use a protractor. Albeit, it may be a bit fuzzy, but I'm sure you could do it if you had to. On the other hand, when was the last time (or first time) that you were encouraged to write down your personal mission statement? Or the values that you want to live by? Or *who* you want to be when you grow up rather that *what*?

Unless you've sought out time to reflect on your own, or had very progressive parents, the first time you've likely ever confronted those Big Life Questions was when you entered Adulthood.

Or maybe, when you picked up this book (yes, we will be going through all those exercises together very, very soon).

I know for myself, the first time I ever asked myself these Big Life Questions was when I was on the precipice of entering the club. It was almost like an entrance exam of sorts. Growing up in my little suburban town filled with carnivals and teachers who had taught my peers *and* their parents, I had never been exposed to anything other than The Path. Combine that with the fact that my parents visibly sacrificed so much for me and my siblings to be *happy* and better off than they were—I knew what I had to do: become the pinnacle of success. And, you can bet I kept my eye on the prize. Well, you all already know how I played the system.

But, there was a little hiccup along the way that shifted *my* path off of *The* Path. During my senior year of college, I realized, almost by accident, that I was on track to graduate a semester early. Partially because I was the biggest high-achieving nerd you could imagine, partially because I had loans to pay, I decided to go for it. This wasn't strategic by any means. But, it did leave me with a major life decision: do I start work a semester before all of my peers to get ahead of the game and start paying off my debt to get to this job in the first place, or do something more introspective (read: riskier)?

When that thought crossed my mind, there was something in me that started to wake up. Because I, like many naïve and ambitious college students saddled with loans to pay and scholarships to live up to, got a bit side-tracked over those four years at school. I arrived on NYU's campus bright-eyed and ready to take on the world. I thought that I could do it all—anything I set my mind to. But, I soon got distracted by the status and money that those Big Important Companies flaunt on campus. And, I got wrapped up in *The Path* before I knew it. After completing a summer internship at that investment bank, I didn't *really* think I would work there. Something just didn't feel right about it. I had big plans to change the world, you know? But, then I saw the money. And, I heard the advice from all the adults in the room. And, I saw how my peers reacted when I told them. So, I accepted the job offer for the following year. It seemed like the right thing to do, even though deep down I knew it wasn't right for me.

So, maybe out of confusion, maybe out of a tiny sense of rebellion I decided to buck the system for the first time in my young life. I made a seemingly random, but extremely important choice. I took some of the money I saved on opting out of that last semester of my expensive education (or more like the $2,000 I had to my name after that summer internship) and used it for another form of learning: I would travel *alone* for those four extra months. Alone. For four months. I was going to backpack around Australia and New Zealand for months with one backpack, all by my lonesome.

It might not seem crazy now, but back in 2013 this type of travel for a twenty-one-year-old girl from the United States was kind of a big deal. I didn't have any role models who did a last-minute switch-up of The Path. Gap years hadn't yet made their way into our cultural conversation (thanks, Malia Obama), and I was born way too long after the casual days of travel in the 1970s. But, for some reason I just had this inner knowing that this choice would be more beneficial, and heck, more fun when it came to my long-term success. I wouldn't necessarily say I was a risk-taker, or quite confrontational by any means back then. Up until that point, I hadn't made any life decisions that required convincing. The decision was made too quickly for anyone around me to opine, because to this day I'm not sure how I convinced anyone—my parents, my future employers at that Very Important Company, and even myself—that this was a good idea. But thankfully, I had stored up some goodwill that no one put up much of a fight.

I went into this four-month excursion thinking that it would be a good way to decompress before starting the rest of my life. I, quite innocently, thought it would be a simple, matter-of-fact trip. I did the whole study abroad thing a few years earlier. NYU kind of forced their students to circle around the globe so they had more housing options for all 40,000 of us, which was lucky for me in hindsight—so I had a couple of passport stamps to my name already. I knew that "travel could change you" and the whole deal we see on Instagram from people like Sally. But,

I couldn't have foreseen the impact this pre-adult honeymoon would have on the rest of my life.

During the course of this book, we'll get into more of my observations and stories from that life-changing trip, but let me simply say for now that those four months in the South Pacific turned my world upside down. Without it, I may have entered Adulthood with a view that everything *is*, in fact, as it seems. I might not have questioned the Adults in the room. I probably would have just accepted that long, boring hours spent behind a desk were going to be the norm for the rest of my life. I might have seen the world in black and white.

But, I didn't. Because, the moment that I stepped off that Qantas airplane, backpack in toe, I took one look at my hostel room and had an "oh shit" moment. I absorbed the complete chaos of my shared space with eight very chill strangers, put my TSA-approved lock away, and breathed in deeply. I realized that my entire world view was about to be rocked, and I decided, for once, to let my rule-abiding mind go with it. In short, I spent four months throwing all those rules out the window, forcing myself to ask and answer those Big Life Questions. I reflected on what I wanted my life values to be, what I was passionate about, and most importantly what I saw the rest of my life panning out to look like—all without the pressure of what I was "supposed" to think.

Basically, I spent time alone with Me for the first time in my twenty-one years on this Earth and was pleasantly surprised with those answers that were hiding inside of me all along.

And, potentially even more importantly, I saw that people, hundreds of them, decided to step off The Path and live a life that they loved. While living out of a backpack for an unknown amount of time wasn't for everyone for sure (heck, it wasn't even for me after a couple of weeks), seeing it up close and personal exposed me to this brand-new mindset: adulthood doesn't have to suck. It doesn't have to be filled with draining commutes and mediocre lunches and piles of laundry you can't seem to find the energy to fold. And most importantly, even if adulthood *is* filled with long commutes and fast-paced lunches and never-ending piles of laundry from time to time, you have the power to shift your perspective about what's possible.

So, when I finally got into this exclusive club upon my return, I was shocked at how much *more* different it was than I expected. I showed up in my big-girl suit, notebook packed away ready to take on this whole new world. But, the Adults weren't having it. They were too busy settling into their very black-and-white lives, thank you very much. They were okay with running to the printer for meetings that didn't really matter, missing their kid's soccer games to send out that one last email, and spending their days negotiating their values.

I took one look around and knew this wasn't for me. Because, I already had something stoked within me. I knew that I didn't have to settle. I saw that *this* version of Adulthood was in direct competition with my answers to those Big Life Questions. I remember staring out of windows all the time during that phase of my life—the floor-to-ceiling ones at the office, the tiny one in my Chelsea apartment, the dirty subway ones—and wondering if *this* was "it." I questioned how the hell I got to this place where I was not happy. Well, where no one was.

And sadly, it didn't feel like anyone else was questioning it. No one was talking about it. They were too taken with planning for meetings years (years!) in advance, or waiting in line at the supermarket, eyes glued to their email inbox. They saw the world in a very binary view: yes/no, black/white, good/bad.

I'm here to tell you: there are many, many more shades than that.

Fun House Mirror Number 3: Time is an infinite resource, they say

Most of us enter Adulthood with a very unique view of time. In the first two decades of our lives, we're so used to our lives being scheduled down to the minute and trained to work toward time-specific goals. But, when we get here life is a lot more fluid. A lot more monotonous. A lot grayer.

Instead of being able to avoid interactions with a frustrating teacher after a few months, we realize we're stuck with our boss . . . forever. We have fewer short-term changes to look forward to, because we're operating in a completely different realm of reality. Whereas before, we were able to mark the passage of time by our school breaks, we now had to schedule our own. It's off-putting, to say the least, and can completely mess with your perception of that achievement we're always seeking.

There was one moment in particular a few months into my early adulting journey that shook me off my monotonous schedule and became a moment I will remember for the rest of my life. It was a simple conversation with someone so far on this path that they spoke to me with almost a deadened urgency, and I couldn't help but take their advice very, very seriously. It impacted me so much, it actually was the very seedling for this book way back when this book wasn't even an idea. This person would never know it, but the regret in their voice continued to stoke that fire within me, and forced me to never waiver my answers to those Big Life Questions.

My first "Very Important Job" was quite unique in that they encouraged us young analysts to meet with the senior leaders on our team for general "catch ups." Although these people's schedules were booked up nearly a year in advance (which I found quite honestly insane), I finally managed to book some time with one of the head honchos. He was a tall, older British man with a soft voice. Everyone on my team seemed extremely intimidated by him, but I could tell he had a soft spot. I had noticed how in a few meetings when everyone reacted as though their lives would end if they didn't resolve an issue, he would stare off into the distance, almost like he couldn't believe that *this* was where he ended up.

Don't get me wrong, he had (and still has) a very important job, truly, where his decisions impact thousands of people around the world. But, I appreciated his sense of grounded reality. One of my biggest areas of confusion when I first entered adulthood was when my colleagues would act like the world was on fire based on one simple email response (hint: it wasn't). This man, we'll call him Todd, always brought a sense of reality to that insulated world and insisted that no, life in fact would not end. We would all be fine.

So, I was quite excited when I got a chance to meet with him. I mean at the time, it felt like I was preparing to talk to a celebrity. No one on my team could believe *I*, a lowly analyst, got one whole hour to talk to Todd. I knew it was a big deal, so I prepared some hard-hitting questions. But, I was not about to waste this precious time with questions about the printer or his predictions for our team structure. I was going to ask him about *life*.

When Todd entered the glass conference room in which we were scheduled to meet, I was already there scribbling away in my notebook. He seemed tired, and although he put on a pretty believable game face, I could tell he was not looking forward to spending an hour feigning excitement about some very basic questions from a twenty-two-year-old.

But, I didn't waste any time. "Todd, you've been working at this company for twenty years. Wow!" I started, visibly a bit nervous. "But, how has your perception of time changed since you were an analyst?"

I asked this question, because one of the things I just could not get over—one of my most confusing trick mirrors in adulthood—was the perception of time. Every time people around me would talk about plans for next year, I would feel my chest tighten. Next year? What about next week? I could barely keep track of what day it was, let alone know what I was planning to do next *year*. What if I wasn't here next year? What if I was in Bali teaching a random yoga retreat like Sally? Who *seriously* knew?!

Todd slowly looked out the window, scratching his beard the moment I asked—like he had been pondering this question for a while. But, instead of answering directly, he said something that shook me to my core. It was exactly what I needed to hear in that moment. And, it made that fire that was lit during my time in the South Pacific grow a little stronger. Todd looked me in the eyes, with a faraway gaze, and said:

> "Katina, time is something that can pass you by so quickly, especially as you get older. But, it's the only resource we have control over. So, don't let it pass you by without doing something to fill it. As an adult, twenty years can be gone in the blink of an eye if you don't watch carefully enough. Well, that's what it does for some of us, anyway. But you're still young. You still have time. Don't blink and let twenty years disappear."

I must have looked like a crazed lunatic as I scribbled down his thoughts, word for word. And, you know—I still have that notebook. When I read it back now, I could almost feel the urgency and regret in his tone. *Don't blink and let twenty years disappear.*

Here's something I realized after that conversation with Todd: twenty years (or ten, or five even) pass by quickly if you're not aware of it. If we don't sit down and ask ourselves those Big Life Questions. If we spend our time negotiating instead of choosing. If we keep acting like The Sims and hiding our fears behind our perfect little houses.

Because, when we start telling the truth, all these trick mirrors seem to shatter right before our eyes. They stop being so scary and instead become clues for our next step. I know it can feel like if we just avoid looking at them, they might just disappear. But trick mirrors never disappear unless we stare them straight in the face. They might be uncomfortable at first, but they can force us to a place where we have to look our distorted, confusing self in the eye and ask, truly: Who the hell am I? Who have I ever been? And, who do I *want* to be?

Before we dive into answering those deep questions, together, over the course of this book the main idea I want you to take away from this glorified vent session is simple: you're not crazy or weird or lonely for feeling some type of way about entering Adulthood. Well, about any big transition in life, really. The majority of us have been taught to think in a linear fashion for the first eighteen years of our lives, at least. There was no room for experimentation or mess-ups or random backpacking trips to the South Pacific. We've been trained not to question the status quo, or authority, or this version of "success" that has been handed down to us from some old white dude generations ago.

And then, it seems that we're dropped in this unfamiliar world, one where everything appears the same but feels completely different than we expected. It's like the curtain fell down and now we're left standing here—all alone and afraid—forced to navigate these nuances of *the rest of our lives* without any help.

So, trust me when I say that the first step toward navigating Adulthood in a mindful, happy, and conscious way is knowing that you're not alone in thinking that things truly are not what they seem. When you run into the bathroom stall at work for what feels like the thousandth time because it feels like you're stuck on a never-ending hamster wheel—you're not alone. When you're waiting on a never-ending line at Trader Joes with a To-Do list racking up in your brain, you're not alone.

So, let's take a deep breath for a moment (literally) and do something a bit counter-intuitive: close our eyes for a moment, and spend just a blink of time alone. You don't need to take a big crazy four-month backpacking trip to Australia or teach yoga in Bali in order to confront these trick mirrors. We're going to work through all the evidence-based tips and tricks in order to shatter these feelings for good, but let's start with just a tiny experiment. Because, when you do, you'll start to see that everything that looks cloudy and weird and confusing becomes a tiny bit clearer.

Okay, ready? Close your eyes for just a moment and take a deep breath. A breath that swirls around your insides and let's go of anything that's stuck. Anything that's holding you back. Anything that feels wrong or bad or confusing. Feel it, and let it go for just a moment.

If you didn't *actually* take a deep breath because you thought it was weird, do it now (did you know I can see you through this book? Kidding). Because, this ride we're on is about to get wilder, and our breath is a tiny aspect of our lives we have complete control over. But before we go any further, let me let you in on a little secret.

— TWO —

Let Me Tell You a Secret

Remember when we were kids, and we would play "make believe"?

For some reason I was never really into watching TV as a kid, save SpongeBob SquarePants, so my free time was often spent in the Land of Make Believe. I would rally anyone I knew to join in. Looking back on my Make Believe games now that I'm older, I realize that they were *pretty* damn boring. We definitely weren't entering magical worlds or pretending that trees were monsters. I didn't lead us into battle or seek out adventure on my makeshift boat. Instead, my fantasy-world followers and I entered the mystical, curious world of Adulthood.

In my pretend world, Adults were basically royalty. To me, I saw them as a real-life version of Angelica's mom from The Rugrats—sporting trendy pencil skirts, yapping on their cell phone, and giving presentations in big, window-filled conference rooms. And, life from that vantage point looked glamorous. So, I visited that future world often. Sometimes, my mom would be my office manager. She was relegated to shuffling papers and pretending to look "busy" while I talked in gibberish on my fancy cell phone (read: Tamagotchi). Other times, I would force my younger siblings to be my students, scribbling away in notebooks, though they barely knew the alphabet yet. The games that I created spanned all aspects of Adulthood, from Tattoo Parlor (it was a time when Milky Pens were a big deal) to Emergency Room Doctor (we had very professional-looking robes and Beanie Babies on our operating table) to Motherhood (my youngest brother might be scarred from the outfits we forced him to wear).

As I look back on my visits to the Land of Make Believe now, I realize that each game had something in common: everyone was very, very busy knowing *exactly* what they were supposed to do. Even though I had no clue what tattoo artists or doctors did during their day-to-day, pretending to be them filled hours of my own. I observed early on that decision-making prowess and confidence were key. Doctors didn't second guess the operations their Beanie Babies needed. Tattoo artists never questioned the permeance of their creations. Teachers never got stumped by a student's question. Moms never thought twice about how to fix the scrape on your knee.

Because from the outside looking in, Adults always knew what the heck to do.

But, let me let you in on a little secret: In real-life Adulthood, no one knows what they're doing.

Fraud Alerts don't just happen to your credit card

You might not see it at first. You might still think that everyone around you is an Expert in Life while you have no clue what the difference between laundry detergent and softener is—let alone how to do your job. Because when you first arrive in The Club, it feels like your black-and-white world slowly turns grey. It's nothing like the Land of Make Believe you imagined it would be as a kid. The Fun House mirrors are everywhere. You don't realize until much later that everyone who looks like they were sprinting towards a destination is merely just moving towards the road that seems the most . . . right. And, all those people who you thought had all the answers suddenly look so . . . human.

Instead, when you first get here you see everyone else as a Very Serious Adult while you're still a kid. You wonder why your team keeps asking *you* to create the presentations for the boss when you can barely figure out how to turn on your computer. You question why your landlord trusts *you* to make rent payments on time when you can't even keep your plants alive. You wonder why the bank increased *your* credit limit when you still buy your coffee with quarters. You feel like you're walking on eggshells everywhere you turn—and one day, one moment someone, somewhere will expose you to be the fraud you think you are deep down.

Because, the scariest part of it all is that someone will finally figure out that you have no clue what you're doing. That you somehow just don't measure up. That you'll never, ever reach your fullest potential since you're already failing at everything it seems. And, walking around with this big, scary secret can sometimes feel the most draining.

Experts call this feeling of pervasive inadequacy Imposter Syndrome. I call it *Fraud Alerts.* Psychologists have found that this temporary state of being, one where you believe you're riding on the curtails of luck instead of your own hard work, is often triggered by adding a new achievement to your book. That achievement, whether that's landing a job, moving to a new city, or entering a new stage of life, can distort our brains to see trick mirrors at every turn.

And, while some lucky ones might feel right at home the moment they enter a new phase of life, the majority of us think we're frauds when we hit a big life turning point. Imposter Syndrome is estimated to affect over 70 percent of adults in the United States alone. And, us Millennials and generations beyond are primed to feel like imposters more than any other generation.

This isn't something we're just making up in our heads. I love the way clinical therapist Cara Maksimow has described how *Fraud Alerts* have become pervasive in the Millennial generation. Cara has said that our generation's upbringing has exposed us (or not) to a variety of factors that encourage a feeling of inadequacy, even when we achieve something great. "Millennials have grown up with the pressures of social comparison, the age of technology, and the beginnings of overprotective helicopter parenting, which contribute to anxiety and fear around work performance. The bar is also set much higher than in the past . . . yet, failure is not something many millennials have experience with."

We will actually dive into the societal reasons as to why we are the way we are in Part II ('cause hey, it's not *all* our fault), but for now we can largely agree that we have been led down a path of least resistance for over two decades—whether that was through our education, our parents, or society at large. Up until we arrive in The Club, we have been confined to a black-and-white world, when in reality, there are millions of shades of grey. And then, we get into The Club, and believe that we're not good enough or smart enough or prepared enough to make Big Life Decisions.

If you're reading this and feel doomed—fear not. First of all, researchers discovered Imposter Syndrome long before us Millennials (and Gen Z, you too) entered adulthood. It's a common human experience that is rooted in our inability to recognize our own achievements. Psychologists Pauline R. Clance and Suzanne A. Imes discovered this state of being back in 1978 when they were trying to understand why high-achieving women were uncomfortable relishing in their own success, and rather, attributed it to luck. Over the years, researchers have realized that this feeling knows no bounds—often, the more outward success you achieve, the more that you doubt your ability to be there.

But, there are ways we can stop calling the Fraud Alert on ourselves. Because, if we live in this mindset for longer than the lease of our first apartment, it can have a real impact on our lives. Trust me, this isn't a mindset that we want to avoid addressing. Since this psychological experience impacts our brain's response to stress, it signals to our brain that we must constantly operate in this fear-based world of self-doubt. Psychologist Dr. Audrey Ervin says that "[Imposter Syndrome] can negatively impact careers because people may overproduce to prove they are capable. This can lead to burnout and ultimately, it will be counterproductive. People may miss opportunities, because they don't feel worthy or capable, despite being competent."

And, these impacts don't simply apply to our professional lives. When we believe that we aren't capable of being real, functioning, competent adults without sacrificing something, everyone around us suffers (plants, landlords, our partners, most importantly ourselves). So, for all of you who, like me, believed that their Type-A, overachieving mindset was what got them this far in the first place, let's stop this negative spiral in its tracks. There is a scientifically-proven way to get out of your own head, and start acting like you're capable of the things everyone else expects of you. I hinted at the answer earlier in this chapter. You high-achieving perfectionists might want to go back and search for it.

But, for the rest of us, here it is again:

In Adulthood, no one else knows what the heck they're doing.

I love the way Dr. Jason Eckerman has described the pull that Imposter Syndrome has on our overall perception of the world: "Part of what makes Imposter Syndrome so powerful," Eckerman says, "is feeling like we're not able to talk about it without exposing ourselves as being a fraud." But, Eckerman goes on to explain that when we break the glass and realize that people we look up to, the so-called Adults in the room, are feeling similar to us—it ends the cycle.

The Magical Moment that broke the spell

Have you ever thought someone was invincible? That they embody everything you want to be?

The moment I started my first job, I saw the most ideal version of my future self sitting just a few cubicles away. She had a badass job that combined making positive impact in the world while also making money, an amazing wardrobe, and emitted a level of confidence that made it seem like she was walking on thin air. She strode around our office floor as if she was wearing a cape of self-assurance, whether it was during a tough meeting or when the coffee machine broke. This woman, we'll call her Candace, was everything I aspired to be.

But, her life couldn't have felt further away from my reality.

I had been walking around in a cloud of confusion for months, and every choice I made—from the crackers I bought at the supermarket to the Excel model I built on my two-screen computer—seemed like the breaking point that would sound the alarm. I believed that soon, everyone would know that I did not belong. There were days when my jet-black Express suit got a bit too uncomfortable, and the worst-case scenario began to play on loop in my head. As I stared at my computer screens, unable to draft a semi-coherent email to Joe in Accounting, I couldn't help but think that everyone who read it would wonder: *How did* she *get here?*

My own experience with Imposter Syndrome was hitting me real hard. I was only a few months into Adulthood, and I had never felt so unworthy of the life that was beginning to take form before me. I didn't understand how everyone else seemed to figure "it" out so quickly—they were all on a mission, walking to the printer or the subway with such direction, such confidence, that I didn't think they would ever understand how scary it felt to not belong. To question their every move. To feel like they were the only ones who got let into The Club by mistake, and any minute some big, scary Security Guard would revoke their admission.

But, oddly enough, seeing Candace as a role model from afar made me feel both capable and inadequate at the same time. She was about ten years my senior, and even though I could so clearly see how I *wanted* my life to turn out, it seemed impossible from my purview that it would ever happen that way.

So, when I went into the bathroom one evening after a long night of hacking away at a stubborn Excel formula, I couldn't have been more surprised. I walked in unsuspectingly, sure that no one else on my team was crazy enough to stay at work this late—in a very uncomfortable suit, no less. But, I was taken aback when I heard sobs coming from the far bathroom stall. Loud, uncontrollable, heaving sobs. Sobs that attempted to turn into a sniffle once the door closed behind me.

I went about my business as quickly as I could, but my curious, naïve self felt the need to call out to my late-night fellow co-worker. "Hey—is everything okay?" I yelled over the running water as I washed my hands, sure that another analyst would exit the stall with a juicy story about the terrible thing their manager said. But, no. There as I was washing my hands on the 20th floor bathroom at 10 p.m. on a Thursday night, my entire world was rocked. Because that moment, I locked eyes with a puffy-eyed, snot-nosed Candace in the mirror.

Candace. Yes, my far-away role model, the invincible woman who seemed so sure, so confident, so clear was having a breakdown late at night in the bathroom stall at work. But, instead of brushing herself off and pretending this whole awkward scenario never happened, Candace did something unexpected: she acknowledged me.

The moment that our eyes met, I wasn't sure what to do. Should I hug her? Apologize? Walk out mid-hand wash and act like I never heard anything? As the potential scenarios were running through my mind, Candace smoothed out her dress and stared back at me in the mirror with a look mixed with raw emotion and gracefulness. My brain searched for something, anything to say to the woman I looked up to the most. But before I could come up with something to lessen the pink flush on my cheeks, Candace put her hand up and shook her head.

"Don't," she said with a tinge of laughter, "don't worry about it. Everyone has messy moments, Hun. You'll see." Candace's eyes were still puffy and red, but smiling at the edges. I still couldn't think of anything to say, though I was almost brought to tears while I thought about my own messy moments as of late.

This moment of shared humanity dissipated as quickly it happened. Candace sniffled a bit, wiped her eyes free of mascara, and looked at me with an almost parental gaze. "What are you doing here so late, anyway?" she asked, curiously. I mumbled something back about Excel and long meetings and not having a life outside of work, anyway. She smiled with a look of knowingness and left the bathroom with her cape of confidence on tight.

She may have never known it, but witnessing Candace's humanness up close was remarkable for me. It gave context to my own confusion. It shed some light on this idea that everyone has a messy moment or two (or seven hundred), but that doesn't necessarily warrant a full-blown fraud alert either.

That heck, we may all feel like imposters at some point in our lives—but that feeling doesn't need to define us. And, from the outside you could seem to have everything figured out, but there are still Thursday nights that warrant a breakdown in the bathroom stall at work.

Now, I'm not saying to seek out encounters that make your mentors cry. But, as Dr. Eckerman says, "Talking with someone who embodies your idea of success can actually help you see things differently." They're able to put things in perspective a bit. Eckerman recommends, "When you're feeling like you don't belong in these situations, it can be helpful to talk with mentors who are more experienced. Many times, we find that other people who we see as deserving often feel the same way, and it can help you realize that what you're feeling is normal."

But, what if I were to tell you that there may be something even bigger here at play? What if Imposter Syndrome largely exists because we're living a life that's not truly our own?

Let me tell you an even bigger secret

The first time I ever truly thought about how I *actually* wanted my life to turn out was on the floor of a high school auditorium in a neighborhood in deep Brooklyn.

It wasn't even my high school. In fact, I was already twenty-two years old. And, if I'm being honest, I wasn't even supposed to be thinking about this question myself. I was meant to be supporting my fourteen-year-old mentee, Maria, as she reflected on her own future goals.

A few months after starting work, I had joined a high school mentoring program through my workplace as a way to get out of my own head. To stay connected with the activities and communities I once loved as I navigated this new world of adulthood. Growing up as a first-generation kid, my parents always enrolled me in free programs that gave me a peek into the future I could have if I worked hard enough (their words, not mine). So, I felt like it was finally my time to be that person for the next bright-eyed tween. But, even though we were only a few weeks into the program, it was consistently proving to teach me more about myself than anything else.

Case-in-point: This simple exercise. I knew that we had an easy task—to draw a picture of yourself in the past, present, and future. But, the teacher's instructions pulsed in my brain: think about what values were important to you and what will be going forward. *Who do you want to be?*

So, as Maria scribbled on her paper and chatted with her friends about normal teenage stuff like college and boys, I zoned out into what felt like the Twilight Zone. *Who did I want to be?* I had never really thought about it before. The answers I had explored during my backpacking trip aside, I only really knew where I wanted to live or work right now. I had been so focused on putting my head down and achieving every milestone that was laid before me, I never really created the space to think about that big picture. I always knew what I had to achieve in the moment. But, who I wanted to be? Other than "a good person," I didn't have any clue.

When I shared my very (very) mediocre drawings with Maria only a few minutes later, I felt my eyes light up for the first time in what seemed like forever. In my "past" bucket, I drew the high-achieving nerd that I always knew myself to be. The girl that is obsessed with collecting the "right" answers—straight A's in school, sports medals galore, loads of friends. My "present" box was nearly the opposite. I drew a lonely figure wearing a very uncomfortable suit (Express, can you hear me yet?) sitting behind multiple computer screens and surrounded by big windows that locked her inside.

My "future" box surprised even myself. But, when I drew it, it felt *so right*. It was something that I always knew deep down I wanted. And, it couldn't be further away from my current reality. I sketched a stick figure woman wearing comfortable pants (very important), on top of a mountain surrounded by fresh air and nature, equipped with a notebook and clearly, a very flexible schedule.

Even though my future self was so far away from the human sitting cross-legged on a high school auditorium floor, bags under her eyes from too much coffee and too little free time, I recognized her immediately. I realized in that moment that it was never my dream to climb the corporate ladder or to go to business school or to collect all this "stuff" that other people expected of me.

Instead, I wanted to live a life that mattered—to me.

This realization launched me into a deep self-exploration process, a process that started to undo all the conditioning that told me what was "right" and "wrong" up until that point. One that allowed me to figure out *who* I wanted to be, not what.

Here's the biggest secret of all, one that we'll break down throughout the rest of this book: when you live a life that's completely aligned with your *own* values, one that's based on your *own* perception of "right," it doesn't matter what other people think. You won't feel like a fraud, like you're not good enough or you don't belong or you got here by mistake, because the standards are set by *you*.

I know, it seems like a lofty goal. It might feel impossible from your very seat right now. But, we are going to work through every single piece of crafting a life in which you are the expert. One where you truly believe that you in fact are worthy and smart and prepared enough to be here.

Our first exercise? The very one that launched me on a path toward living a value-led life: Draw your future you.

The instructions are simple. You don't need to be an artist by any means. These answers don't need to be perfect. This might be the first time in your life where there's no "right" or "wrong" answer you're searching for. Our purpose here is to really understand what ideas or principles drove you up until this point, what you believe is most important to you right now, and looking forward, *who* you want to be. This exercise will set the stage for much of our work together throughout the rest of this book, because we're starting to touch the tip of the Reflecting Iceberg. We're starting to ask ourselves those Big Life Questions, such as: What are your values? Have they changed over the course of your life? And, as we start to exercise this muscle, we'll be able to tap into it even more over time.

So, roll up your sleeves and get ready to peel back some layers. Some questions you might ask yourself: What values had you been raised with? What was important to 14-year-old You? What's driving you now? Without any rules, what's important to you looking ahead?

Take a couple of moments to pause here and scribble away. Feel free to draw (or scratch out some stick figures) directly in this book or on any scraps of paper you have nearby. Keep it simple and reflect from your gut.

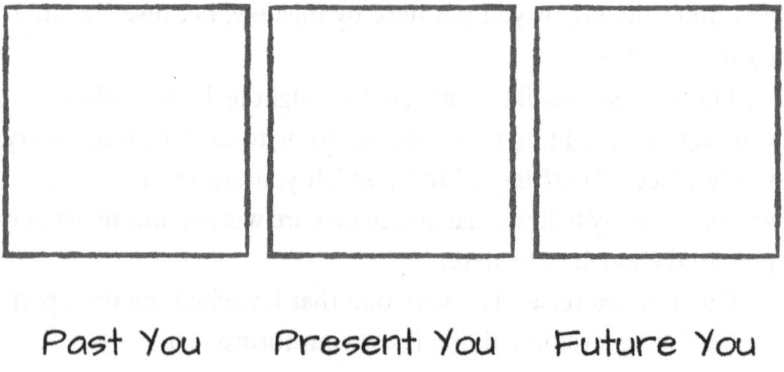

After you've taken a couple of moments to move through this simple exercise, think about if there are a couple of words or phrases to describe your Future You and the values you want to live by. Is it flexibility or structure? Adventure or comfort? Maybe it's all or none of the above. These words are likely somewhere deep in your bones already; you don't need to overturn too many rocks to get there. Simply jot down what first comes to mind; we'll come back to these words later when we begin mapping out our lives in Part Three.

Now, if this exercise was difficult for you, trust me, you're not alone. I've done this exercise with hundreds of people, and most have struggled at first, too. As we've learned, there are many societal reasons why we Millennials (and anyone over the age of twenty, honestly) haven't been taught to tune into our values. We've been taught to follow The Path and never question it. We've been trained to listen to the rules—and never break them—for a variety of reasons, from the way that our human brains are wired to the way society was structured when we were kids. We didn't get to this point by accident.

And, I'm about to show you why.

Part Two:

You're Not Here by Accident (Even If You Wish It Were So)

Reality leaves a lot to the imagination.
-John Lennon

THREE

It's Not (Fully) Your Fault

Back in the day, did you ever get in trouble for using your outdoor voice?

Maybe it was in your childhood classroom after a particularly engaging lesson. Maybe it was after your mom had *enough* of you fighting with your younger brother. Maybe it was when you were actually following all of the rules on the playground, but got a little too excited.

After hearing The Rules enough times—*be quiet, calm down, don't raise your voice*—you stopped speaking up. You stopped yelling and cheering and expressing yourself fully. Maybe you didn't even notice, but the impact that following those rules had on your long-term decision-making is enormous. Honestly think about it for a moment: when was the last time you got loud, just for the heck of it?

I know after the age of seventeen, I rarely raised my voice above an inside decibel. It wasn't like I consciously limited myself to hushed tones, but I certainly didn't shout in any public setting, even when I was angry. I had been conditioned over the years by my parents, my teachers, and society writ large that the "right" way to handle myself when I felt any stirring emotion was to be quiet. To smile and take a breather. To keep my outside voice to a minimum, because that's not how adults act.

I'm not saying that these lessons are all bad. Certain rules in society are important for us to function in a connected, wholesome way. Naturally, yelling for the sake of yelling is *not* good. Researchers have found that growing up in a household where parents use yelling as a form of discipline can increase the risk of their children developing psychological issues, like depression or anxiety later in life. Yelling used as a form of punishment has a similar impact to any other type of abuse (I'm sure when my New York City-raised mother whose normal voice is a scream reads this, she won't be pleased).

But, the concept that I'm talking about here is subtler. It's not just about being able to yell at someone when you're angry. It's about how we've been unconsciously taught across many areas of our lives to act in a certain way based on what people think is "right." Those lessons—*be quiet, calm down, don't raise your voice*—among many others guide a plethora of other decisions we make as adults, even if we don't realize it.

There's a baby in your brain

What if I told you that part of your brain, the part that we think of as our most logical self, is simply just taking orders from a toddler?

I'm being a little facetious here, but you catch my drift. Part of our brain, our conscious-thinking part, only accounts for about ten percent of our daily interactions. This came as a major surprise to me. I always considered myself a reflective, logical person who was completely in charge of her life. So, when I learned that the way I was living my life was largely driven by beliefs I didn't even know I had, I was confused. But here's something even more shocking: even though we think we're actively making all of our life choices, our unconscious brain is driving our thoughts behind the scenes without us even realizing it.

If you recall, I never ended up following through with my Emergency Room Doctor dream, so I'm going to keep this part really, really simple. From here on out, we'll call our unconscious brain our Baby Brain. I'll be honest, this is very much oversimplifying the complexities of our human brain, but for the sake of our learnings here we'll keep it straightforward. Our Baby Brain has one job: to keep us safe. Modern neuroscience is finding that our unconscious mind, the only part of our brain that is fully developed from the moment we were born, takes care of a lot more than our breathing or digestion like we're taught in middle school biology. Our Baby Brain has been with us from Day 1—taking in all the sights and sounds we've been exposed to without us even realizing it. It absorbs subtle cues that our conscious mind can't see and develops opinions on our favorite color or political party that guide our day-to-day actions. You can imagine your Baby Brain as a little note-taking minion, feeding your conscious mind a tiny summary each day of all the work it's doing behind the scenes.

But, there's always a catch, right? Each time we have an experience, good or bad, our Baby Brain collects it as a data point. It doesn't judge the impact that data point will have out in the real world. Take this as an example: if you ever broke a bone after jumping off the top of the jungle gym as a kid, your Baby Brain stored information to stay away from jumping or jungle gyms or maybe both. But, if you received a lot of attention after breaking said bone (having a cast in elementary school was a *big* deal), your Baby Brain may have taken in another piece of information: when I'm sick or hurt, people pay attention to me.

And, sometimes the wires get crossed in the process. Our Baby Brain then feeds that information to our conscious mind, which has the ability to judge its validity. But, when we're living in autopilot mode, our conscious mind doesn't even recognize the influence our Baby Brain might have. Take it from the father of analytical psychology, Carl Jung: "Subliminal aspects of everything that happens to us may *seem* to play very little part in our daily lives. But they are the almost invisible roots of all our conscious thoughts."

So, next time you find yourself gravitating toward a job description on LinkedIn or even a person at the bar and you have no idea why, take a step back for a moment. Your Baby Brain is likely dictating your decision-making without you even realizing it. Think about it: every single decision, from tiny ones like deciding to spend money on coffee every day to big ones, like who you choose as your life partner, are colored by subconscious experiences, stories, and observations. As best-selling author and badass scientist, Leonard Mlodinow, puts it, "We believe when we choose a laptop or laundry detergent, plan a vacation, pick a stock, take a job, assess a sports star, make a friend, judge a stranger, and even fall in love, we understand the principle factors that influenced us. Very often, nothing could be further from the truth. As a result, many of our most basic assumptions about ourselves and our society are false." In other words, we *think* we're in charge of our decisions in life, but often they're automatic. All along, our Baby Brains have been collecting information in stealth mode throughout our lives in order to create our own bounds of decision-making. Our own rules of "right" and wrong. Our own perceptions of reality.

It can be difficult to accept that invisible forces have been guiding everything in our lives so far. Heck, it might feel like you're in a weird science fiction movie or something. But, neuroscientists, psychologists, and economists alike are now discovering that we humans are not as rational as we liken ourselves to be. Research proves that our environment—both past and present—determines much of the "conscious" decisions that we make.

It's not all bad news; we *do* have the ability to shift our Baby Brains if we actively stop living in autopilot mode.

So, who cares if we have babies living in our brains?

Maybe you're a little miffed at the fact that we seem to have a lot less control over our lives than we imagine we do. I don't blame you. It's a hard pill to swallow. So, why am I telling you all of this stuff in the first place? If our Baby Brains control our lives anyway, what does it all matter?

Well, when we're living in autopilot mode, running on the work-gym-sleep hamster wheel every day, our Baby Brains *do* have complete control over our lives. But, the moment that we become awake to how much of an impact our unconscious mind has on our lives we can begin *adulting* in a way that we choose, instead of negotiating the life we're expected to live. First, it's important to recognize that there are influences beyond your control that have shaped what you want to be when you grow up. There are reasons that are bigger than you behind why you might have felt like a fraud when you first arrived in Adulthood, or why it seems like there are trick mirrors at every turn. It's not *fully* your fault.

Now, we can soak in this learning for a moment, but know that it doesn't allow us to release all responsibility. We aren't going to wallow in our self-pity, because we chose to go to a college with a fancy-sounding name before we knew a thing about what the campus was like. Or maybe we accepted a job based on the toys our parents bought us as kids instead of what actually made us excited. Because, even though our Baby Brains color every decision we make, we *can* game the system. We know for a fact that our decisions up until this point are purely based on the information your Baby Brain has been collecting for decades. That should make you feel a little better. What might make you feel great? We can keep feeding our Baby Brains more information, collecting more data points, in order to make those unconscious decisions more aligned with the values we want to live by.

Depending on who you talk to, some people call the way our Baby Brains work unconscious thought, and others call them *limiting beliefs*. These limiting beliefs—or that little voice in our head that guides our behavior by telling us we're not good enough, smart enough, prepared enough—can impact our decision-making greatly. Imposter Syndrome is a classic case of our Baby Brain taking full control over our perceived reality. Of course, our Baby Brains aren't always bad. In fact, our unconscious minds are immensely powerful and often guide us toward decisions that our conscious brain could never conceive of. But, the problems happen when we're not at all aware that these limiting beliefs can make us feel less than we're capable of, because of the data points that our Baby Brains have collected throughout our lives.

Don Miguel Ruiz, a prolific thinker and writer, explains the limiting beliefs that our world projects onto us from the moment we take our first breath in his novel, *The Four Agreements*. Ruiz calls this process of learning to operate in our world as the *domestication of humans*. He explains that from the time we're children, we're taught what type of behavior is acceptable based on what we observe from our parents, at school, at church, from television. We are taught to live through a system of punishments and rewards—so much so, that we come to live in fear of not getting the reward, or attention of our parents, teachers, or siblings. We are trained to want the reward so badly, to fear what will happen if we *don't* get the reward, "we start pretending to be what we're not, just to please others, just to be good enough for someone else."

You can see how this domestication, this training of our Baby Brain, becomes a problem, right? How when we begin to act from a place of fear, we don't know the difference between who we are and who we're acting like. Take a moment to scratch your brain and think about the values we just reflected on last chapter in relation to how Ruiz describes our personal belief systems: "Eventually we become someone we're not. We become a copy of Mamma's beliefs, Daddy's beliefs, society's beliefs . . . the domestication is so strong, at a certain point in our lives we no longer need anyone to domesticate us. We are so well trained that we are our own domesticator."

There have been plenty of times in my life, and I'm sure you can think of your own, when I created a punishment for myself without anyone else's input. There have been overt instances like getting a "bad" grade on a test and putting myself on lockdown in my room for days, even though my parents barely batted an eyelash. Or less clear ones, like when I made an awkward comment at a bar to a friend of a friend, and my silly Baby Brain replayed it hundreds of thousands of times, wondering if said person now hated me. Whether we realize we're doing it or not, we create prisons in our own minds of what we *should* and *should not* be doing, which impacts the way we see the world.

There are lots of voices in your head

The first time I realized there was more than one voice in my head, I thought there was something wrong with me. I was seventeen, the same age that I stopped using my outdoor voice. I had finally listened to that old soccer coach of mine, and turned to a new activity during moments of crisis (which, in my teenage years, felt like every day): running. Whenever I would get into an argument with my mom or boyfriend or a catty girlfriend would misinterpret my AIM message, I'd lace up my sneakers and head outside. What started with two (very difficult) miles soon became five. Seven. Nine. My sneakers became my barrier, and my alone time on those concrete roads, swirling through the suburban streets became my safe haven.

At first, the voices in my head started off the same. It was just one that sounded low and loud, almost like it was on a constant loop of incessant nagging. That voice—the only one I had ever been consciously aware of—fed me all the ideas I *expected* to hear. She told me the shitty things were going to get shittier: my legs were tired. It was too cold or too hot or too nice to be on a run. She instilled in me the beliefs that everyone around me, my parents, my school, society in general, had layered on top of me for years. Depending on the day, I would hear the following messages over and over again: I was ungrateful (my mom). I was selfish (my then-boyfriend). I wasn't any fun (my so-called friends). You know, seventeen-year-old stuff. But, for so long, I believed her. My Baby Brain tricked me into thinking I was someone that I wasn't.

Until one day. One day, like nearly every other, I started my run out of pure need. I had just gotten into a major blow-out fight with my mom over something I can no longer remember (isn't it always that way?), and turned to the only solution I could think of: lacing up my sneakers. Of course, as soon as I got moving my Baby Brain rattled off every reason why I *shouldn't* keep going, why I was too tired and hot and angry. She reinforced all the mean comments my mom made just a few moments earlier out of her own anger, yelling at me just like my mom did. But then, as I was about to turn the corner and head back home on my memorized route, another voice piped up. This one was quieter, more confident. She spoke at a volume just above a whisper—but was so clear: "You're okay. You can keep going."

My Baby Brain was so caught off guard, I almost whipped my head around to look for where this voice came from. But, my body knew. It skipped the turn to go home, and kept going at a steady pace while my Baby Brain figured out what the heck was going on. My "best friend" had made her first, conscious appearance, and I thought that I was officially going crazy. But, it felt so right, so good at the same time, that I kept going.

Over time, I'd come to learn that this older, wiser Me, this new voice in my head, was also *me*. Interestingly, this voice was my true self, one that was not layered with all the stuff society pressed on me from the time I was a kid. She wasn't mean. She wasn't selfish. She wasn't a bad friend. This version of me, the real me, was honest and kind and thoughtful. She was patient and understanding. She listened intently and answered fairly. She was my truest, best self.

It took many, many Best Friend dates for me to unwind all of those layers of who my Baby Brain told me I was. It took years to quiet that other voice and approach her with curiosity instead of frustration. And hey, if I'm being honest it's a continuous unraveling process that I don't think ever ends for us humans. But, the moment that we become aware of that voice, the one who is quiet and clear and true, we can start to make decisions for ourselves that keep us in charge.

So right now, we're going to confront all these voices in our head, ones we may not even have realized we have, head on. Yes, right now. Not on a long run that we'll never get to, or during a journaling session years in the future. One of my other favorite thinkers of our time, Michael Singer, the writer behind the Oprah-approved book, *The Untethered Soul*, has described the importance of getting to know the other voices in our head like this: "There is nothing more important to true growth than realizing you are not solely the voice of the mind—you are the one who hears it." So, let's take a couple of minutes to become aware of this controlling little Baby

Brain and the data points it's been collecting all along so we can begin to move forward, consciously.

You'll need a paper and a pen, as well as a timer (yes, a phone works perfectly), and an open mind. This exercise might bring up some stuff for you—stuff that might not be fully resolved in this moment. So, as Singer reminds us: "If you want to be happy, you have to let go of the part of you that wants to create melodrama. This is the part of you that thinks there's a reason not to be happy." Simply allow yourself to move through the process without judgement or letting your Baby Brain interrupt too much. And, whether it's happiness, fulfillment, success, or just living a good, normal Adult life, tap into those values you brainstormed last chapter so we can let that melodrama shit go.

In the space below, give yourself thirty seconds or so to list out *every label you've ever associated with yourself.* For example, it might be "smart" or "pretty" or "weird" or "needy." Who knows. There's no rules or judgment here. These labels don't even need to make sense. Our purpose is to look clearly at all the data points, all the limiting beliefs, our Baby Brains have picked up throughout the years, and see them clearly instead of allowing them to fester without our knowledge. Ready? Go.

Part 2 of this exercise is this: Give yourself a couple of moments to distance yourself from this brain dump. Take a breather, close your eyes, get a glass of water. This stuff is hard and weird; we're beginning to peel back the layers we were never taught to look at. Acknowledge that it might bring up some stuff that feels uncomfortable.

When you're ready, take a look back at that list. There may be thirty random words on there, or three. Now, read each one carefully. Do they make sense to you? Do you feel that some of them are actually true—or bogus? Circle the ones that resonate deeply—positive or negative—and cross off the ones that seem random, irrelevant, or illogical. Maybe they made sense at one point, but no longer apply to who you are right now. Maybe they seem completely out of place. Whatever the reason, in the words of Singer, let that shit go.

We'll come back to this list, along with the values you brainstormed a few chapters ago, many times in our future reflections. But for now, let this sink in. Let it also be clear that a lot of stuff in your life up until this point is not (fully) your fault. It's a compilation of your environment, the rules you've been told (consciously or unconsciously), and the societal ideas you've picked up. And, you're starting to see how they play out in real life—in labels and beliefs you may not have even realized you had.

Now that we've spent some time understanding the factors that drive our behavior on a personal, individual human level, let's look at how society shapes our decision-making. How we've been trained to seek the "right" answers from the time we're kids. How the Dream of the World, as Ruiz calls this Baby Brain stuff, has influenced our own personal dreams without us even recognizing it.

And most importantly, what we can do about it.

—— FOUR ——

Trophies, Awards, and Lies, Oh My!

Back in the day, did you fill your bedroom with collectibles?

The early '90s was a *vibrant* time. If your childhood bedroom looked anything like mine, there was an abundance of Spice Girl lollipop stickers, Pokémon Cards, and Beanie Babies in plastic cases. (Who honestly told us they would be worth millions one day? Mine are currently sitting in my parents' attic, collecting dust.) T-Ball trophies and the coveted Goosebumps book series lined the shelves. NSYNC posters stuck on the walls, but nothing shone as brightly as the neon star stickers that dotted the ceiling.

Growing up, my parents tried *really* hard to help me and my siblings fit into the ultimate suburban, American life. Their childhoods were much different. My dad grew up in a small fishing village in Greece before moving to a one-bedroom apartment in Brooklyn with his loud, large Greek family as a teenager. We often heard stories from his younger years that seemed as though they were out of an ancient movie of him running around barefoot in the cobblestone streets of Koroni, his hometown of 298 people.

The first time he saw a bicycle as a ten-year-old, his mother broke it into four pieces so his siblings wouldn't fight. And then there were tales of him navigating the New York City transit system to get to school without speaking an ounce of English. He would recount these experiences wistfully, as if to teach us a lesson when we whined that it was too cold to walk to the bus stop outside of our house.

My mom, on the other hand, grew up in Flushing, Queens—a curly-haired, Jewish girl in the heart of the Big City. She was mainly raised by her mother, who worked full-time at a hospital, and was a tough woman who didn't put up with shit. My mom and her friends spent their afternoons and weekends hanging out on the block, making up games like "Hit the Stick" or playing jacks or hopscotch to entertain themselves. They knew they had only one rule to follow: don't bother the adults until dinnertime. And, my mom made sure to remind me and my siblings how strictly she and her neighbors followed these rules when we would complain about being bored after five minutes spent outside.

I know that everyone feels as though their parents' childhoods seem like worlds away from their own. Yet, no matter if your parents were fresh-off-the-boat immigrants or fifth-generation Texans, there seemed to be something different in the water when the Millennial generation (and Gen Z, you too) was born. Call it what you want, but there was a cultural shift, one that forced our parents to shuttle us from dance lessons to soccer practice to academic tutoring—even if they'd never even heard the word "extracurricular" until they enrolled you in kindergarten. There was a societal change that made adults feel like all of us kids deserved a trophy just for showing up. And, that shift has impacted the way that *we* see the world and how we interact in it as we enter adulthood.

Lori Gottlieb, a psychotherapist and renowned columnist at *The Atlantic*, noticed this shift back in 2011. She began taking stock of the clients that were entering her therapy practice more frequently, and realized they all had something in common: from the outside, their lives seemed great. Take one of her patients, who she calls Lizzie, for example. She had "'awesome' parents, two fabulous siblings, supportive friends, an excellent education, a cool job, good health, and a nice apartment. She had no family history of depression or anxiety." But, Lizzie couldn't figure out why she "just wasn't happy." Sound familiar?

Gottlieb realized it wasn't just Lizzie. A plethora of her patients, outwardly successful 20- and 30-somethings, would often come to her with mysterious feelings of lack. Of wondering why they felt "less amazing than [their] parents had always told [them] they were." Of being "so indecisive, afraid of making a mistake, unable to trust [their] instincts and stick to [their] choices."

In her now-viral 2011 article, *How to Land Your Kid in Therapy*, Gottlieb describes her observations about millennials who were just beginning to enter the workforce. She posits why their struggles as they entered adulthood—with finding and committing to a career, creating meaningful relationships, and generally just feeling an overall lack of purpose—seemed different than those of generations before.

Gottlieb lands on a few different answers for why these trends are taking place, largely centered on the idea that, "what seems to have changed in recent years, though, is the way we think about and define happiness." When I read her reflection, it struck me at my core. I could have been one of Gottlieb's patients when I was "going through it." I was someone who had it all put together on the outside, but when I got to adulthood, I realized that I *just wasn't happy*. I was someone who had been promised the Ultimate Dream once I arrived in this fabled land, the dream of unwavering, existential happiness, but when I finally arrived, this so-called happiness felt much different than I expected it to feel. So, I followed the advice of modern-day gurus like Gretchen Rubin and Deepak Chopra to keep searching for "it": I made the lists, wrote in the gratitude journals, and experimented with meditation. But, it wasn't until I looked under the hood—until I questioned *what* I was actually searching for—that I understood there was an inherent issue with the way our generation, our society, perceived success in adulthood.

Because for most of us, the goal was to find *happiness* in every area of our lives—always and forever. Gottlieb explains: "Nowadays, it's not enough to be happy—if you can be even happier. The American Dream and the pursuit of happiness have morphed from a quest for general contentment to the idea that you must be happy at all times and in every way." One of the most interesting examples of this cultural shift is Gottlieb's analysis of *The Happiness Project*, a book by Gretchen Rubin that came out around the time this article was published back in 2011. It was topping bestseller charts and encouraging seemingly happy people to optimize their search for this ever-elusive feeling.

At one point in *The Happiness Project*, Rubin writes: "I am happy . . . but I'm not as happy as I should be." Gottlieb's observation of Rubin is quite eye-opening: "How happy should she be? Rubin isn't sure . . . but she sounds exactly like some of my patients. She has two wonderful parents; a 'tall, dark, and handsome' (and wealthy) husband she loves; two healthy, 'delightful' children; a strong network of friends; a beautiful neo-Georgian mansion on the Upper East Side; a law degree from Yale; and a successful career as a freelance writer." But, Gottlieb goes on: "Still, Rubin writes, she feels 'dissatisfied, that something [is] missing.' So, to counteract her 'bouts of melancholy, insecurity, listlessness, and free-floating guilt,' she goes on a 'happiness journey,' making lists and action items, buying three new magazines every Monday for a month, and obsessively organizing her closets." And, even though Gretchen Rubin approaches her search for happiness much like I did when I was "going through it"—trained as a Type-A, overachieving human—she still struggles. "In some ways," Rubin writes in her book, "I'd made myself less happy." Then she adds, citing one of her so-called Secrets of Adulthood, "Happiness doesn't always make you feel happy."

We have created a happiness-obsessed world—one that is fueled by the never-ending options of the Internet, a culture of over-excited parenting, an education system that prioritizes college attendance over personal exploration, and a society that strives for perfection over contentment. But, us Millennials and kids growing up in this modern world today have never actually been taught to understand what happiness truly means—only to delay gratification, shy away from discomfort, and seek it in material, external ways.

So, we're not here by accident.

The rest of this chapter will take us through the cultural shifts that led to us Millennials becoming the entitled, lazy, anxious, ungrateful, purpose-driven, freedom-seeking humans that everyone else makes us out to be (trust me, I'm with you in fighting against those stereotypes, but stick with me). Most importantly though, we'll begin to question how we can shift our mindset and perception of "success" so that we aren't looking for happiness in Ivy League degrees and the *perfect* partner, only to find that we're still seeking that ever-elusive feeling when we seem to have it all.

The operating system is broken

We've all heard the quote: "It's about the *journey*, not the *destination*." To this day, experts are not exactly sure who gifted us such poignant words (is it Ralph Waldo Emerson or a Sunday School teacher from Minnesota?). Nevertheless, this reminder has been plastered everywhere from Pinterest boards to murals on the wall at your office; you can find it on your high school friend's Instagram caption after a long trip or painted gently over the entryway to your doctor's office. Anonymous, half-hearted, aspirational quotes like these could be our generation's tagline. This one's my personal favorite: "Shoot for the moon—even if you miss, you'll land among the stars."

But, even though these Home Goods-inspired reminders encourage us to live in the moment, growing up we were trained to think that the moon—not just the stars—*was* actually within our reach. And frankly, it seemed like reaching the moon was simple. I remember this message was often drilled into my mind: "If you do what you love, you'll never have to work a day in your life," where work was defined as something that we were lucky enough to experience all day every day, not that façade for bill-paying and hours spent behind a computer screen. Ultimate, never-ending happiness seemed attainable to us, no matter what our upbringing was. Whether you were a kid whose immigrant parents struggled to help them achieve the Great American Dream like me or you were enrolled in a fancy private school since you were three, happiness and success seemed to live in the aspirational quotes written on notes in our lunch box or the promise of a college degree. Our parents, teachers, coaches, babysitters, and even TV role models convinced us that yes, you in fact *could* be happy all the time—once you made it into adulthood.

But, this overarching message we continued to receive from all fronts, while admirable on the face of it, was rotting at its core. Barry Schwartz, a professor of social theory at Swarthmore College, says that, "Happiness as a goal is a recipe for disaster." Instead, he offers, "Happiness as a byproduct of living your life is a great thing." When I reflected on that concept, though, it made me think: How often were we actually taught to live our lives regardless of the end goal, experiencing the ebbs and flows of the journey instead of engineering it for perfection? Even though we were often told to "enjoy the journey," our lives were always driving toward the destination instead.

This happiness-as-the-goal-oriented way of living started with a shift in parenting toward the end of the twentieth century. Therapists and teachers alike reflect on the idea that parents today will do anything to avoid their kids being mildly uncomfortable. Paul Bohn, a psychiatrist at UCLA, often witnesses the actions that parents take on behalf of their kids so that they don't need to experience "anything less than pleasant." And, I hate to admit it, but I was no stranger to this form of parenting. Even though my parents moved to the suburbs after I was born—and definitely, *definitely* weren't the recipients of this parenting style themselves—they tried their hardest to create a life of comfort for me and my siblings. When it came to navigating a "bad" teacher or test grade, my parents got involved (even if they were rolling their eyes at how "kids these days" were raised).

But it wasn't just the way my parents raised me, or even the culture in our very middle-class, Long Island enclave. Experts have been trying to understand the effects of highly-engineered parenting for decades after the term "helicopter parenting" was coined in 1990. And, they've found that this cultural shift was largely driven by changes to our nation's economic status, governmental policies, and societal factors that were way beyond our individual control.

Economists Matthias Doepke and Fabrizio Zilibotti have found that as our world became increasingly unequal, parents who had gone to public schools and spent evenings playing kickball in their neighborhoods—like my own—began monitoring their kids' homework and chauffeuring them to activities. Doepke and Zilibotti point to a clear economic shift in the Western world: we went from "permissive parenting" in the 1970s, because there wasn't much of a gap between what someone could earn with or without a college degree, to "helicopter parenting" as inequality increased sharply, and the earning potential between white-collar and blue-collar workers became drastic in the 1980s.

But, this new form of deeply ironic parenting, one that pushed us kids toward a life of delayed gratification while simultaneously rewarding every tiny choice we made through trophies and awards, wasn't the only crack in our collective upbringing. As much as we love to hate on our parents, our education system and a lifetime of schooling catered to obtaining a fancy college degree had a major impact on our perception of happiness as well.

Us Millennials, and the generations following, will have some of the largest percentages of college-educated humans among our ranks. As compared to less than twenty-five percent of our parents, thirty-nine percent of Millennials have a degree from a four-year college or higher. Like Doepke and Zilibotti found in their research, worldwide economic shifts starting in the 1980s signaled the ever-growing importance of obtaining a college degree. That's why, as the Millennial generation began to enter the education system, standardized testing became mainstream. And so, from a young age, our success was consistently rewarded with external validation.

If you were like me, you may have caught yourself (or still do catch yourself) saying: Once this test / basketball season / college application / fill in the blank is over, I can relax. I can enjoy myself. I can *be happy*. I know in my case, as a kid I always found a reason to continue working toward the Next Best Thing. Once I achieved something—whether it was an A on a French project or making the varsity soccer team—I took a quick breath and was on my way forward. I was never taught, and barely encouraged, to live in my success and even find *happiness* in the achievements I was racking up. Even though I knew being happy and "successful" later in life was the end goal, I was surrounded by the mentality of achieving more, being more, striving for more. We were all constantly reaching for the moon, even in the most basic circumstances.

Do you remember the episode in Aziz Ansari's 2015 show, *Master of None*, when his character, Dev, wants a taco for lunch? It's one of my favorite scenes from this show, one that depicts our generation and the world we're operating in so well. Dev lives in New York City, and instead of moseying over to a local taco restaurant, of which there are many, he spends about an hour searching through Yelp, Eater, Foursquare, any other obscure blog he could manage, and even texting his friends for their recommendations to find "The Best Taco" in New York. All the while, he becomes hungrier and hungrier, delaying his seemingly simple lunch in a quest for the moon—the most delicious taco available to him. When Dev finally found *the* taco place, and trekked all the way there, he discovers that it closed just an hour before. Out of hunger and frustration, Dev yells: "This is supposed to be the best taco! What am I supposed to do now? Go eat the second-best taco like some kind of asshole?"

This conundrum so ridiculously and poignantly describes the irony of our generation. We delay gratification—whether for a lunchtime taco or while we're jumping to the Next Best Thing—even though we are never actually satisfied with any of it. Interestingly, there have been many studies in the past few decades that demonstrate when kids are taught to *delay gratification*, they are more "successful" as they get older. Some researchers even say that the ability to delay gratification is the key characteristic to finding success in health, work, and life. In 1972, a famous researcher and Stanford University professor, Walter Mischel, and his team tested hundreds of four- and five-year-old kids with a very simple experiment. They simply brought the children into a private room and gave them two choices: they could eat the marshmallow on the table in front of them right now, or they could wait until the researcher comes back in a few minutes and they'd get two marshmallows instead of one.

But, their findings didn't happen in those fifteen minutes of the experiment. The Stanford researchers kept in touch with these children for over forty years and continued to compare their life outcomes to that fateful choice as a five-year-old: do I eat the marshmallow now or later? Mischel and his team found that those kids who waited for the researchers to return ended up having higher SAT marks, lower levels of obesity, and better scores on a variety of life measures that the researchers had previously determined.

But, as I sat back and absorbed these research findings, I realized that they had one major flaw: who is defining "success"? If it's in the same box as our education system in the Western world, or within the confines of obsessive helicopter parenting, does that mean developing the skill of delaying gratification allows us to keep searching for that ever-elusive happiness? Will we all end up like Gretchen Rubin—with a beautiful New York City apartment, degrees from Ivy League institutions, a healthy family—and still feel like we can be *happier*?

So, what do we do if ultimate happiness isn't the end goal?

When I first entered this crazy world of Adulthood, and I was "going through it," I kept a journal. I called it my Happiness Journal, inspired á la Gretchen Rubin. It was just a basic, Moleskin notebook, but I would stash it away in my bag and secretly take it out at work or on the subway—writing away feverishly whenever I had a moment of confusion (many) or felt a tiny glimmer of happiness (rarely). I felt very Elizabeth Gilbert in *Eat Pray Love*, except I was having a mid-life crisis at twenty-two instead of forty-two.

I mostly just couldn't wrap my head around the idea that I had worked *so hard* to get Here—a place where I *wasn't happy* (I wrote that word-for-word in my Happiness Journal on a late-night subway ride back to my apartment from work). I also felt extremely guilty, because I knew how much my parents had sacrificed for so long in order to get me to a place that made me feel like shit every day. I felt ungrateful. Unworthy. And, like I was the only one who magically arrived in adulthood, ready to have happiness bestowed upon me, and like the Golden Snitch from Harry Potter, it was nowhere to be found.

After a lot of my own personal searching, I realized that the operating system was broken. I came to the understanding that what I was searching for was completely backwards. That happiness as an end-goal, forever and always, was completely unattainable. That I was setting myself up for failure before I even started. I had to look at how I could stop performing for the sake of others—how I could literally stop collecting trophies, or reaching for that new job, or Next Best Thing—and actually be happy with myself without having a reason to be. Not continuously seeking the happiest, just simply happy. Fulfilled. Content.

Even more importantly, I had to—we all have to—recognize that this human experience is filled with many emotions: happiness, sadness, fulfillment, disappointment. And, that in order to actually *feel* them, I would have to stop delaying gratification (or emotion in general) until I achieved something. I would have to look within myself, not to the layers of trophies and awards and achievements I've collected, in order to prove that I was worthy of feeling my feelings.

Shefali Tsabary, PhD, is a clinical psychologist and author whose work focuses on integrating Eastern and Western belief systems and understands how feelings work very, very well. Her perspective on them is enlightening, in fact. In an interview, she describes our feelings as such: "Feelings are a wave, a cascading wave, and you can allow them to come because they're a temporary state of being. The feeling is not you. When we get anxious about our anxiety, we're actually telling it that we've bought into it." And, this doesn't just go for feelings that are categorically difficult. Dr. Tsabary goes on: "Happiness, even, is transient. Life is complex—so you're going to have an ebb and flow of many feelings. You are your inner sense of worth, which will never be touched or varnished by momentary lapses of other people's judgements of or their acceptance. You exist independent of your feelings. Let the feelings come."

So, let's let the feelings freakin' come. That might be the motto of this book. My favorite aspect of Shefali's observation about the human experience is this: our feelings, our validation trophies, our worries and fears and happiness are *not us*. They are experiences that shape us, but they do not define us. And, they come and go throughout life. We are not searching for them under pillows or underneath our graduation caps. Our true worthiness begins deep inside—right at the point where our Baby Brain diverges and our inner voice begins.

There's no sense in searching for *the happiest* when we can be happy (or sad or confused or all three) at any moment, starting right now.

Before we move on, let's take a moment to feel the feelings that are coming up in this moment. Throughout the rest of our time together, we're going to do a lot of exercises that force us to go deep, to confront those feelings that swell up behind our eyelids or in our chest all too often. We're going to be reflecting on why we feel a certain way and what made us do so. But at the moment, we're simply going to practice acknowledging our feelings in the right now, instead of waiting for the Next Best Thing to come along.

So, pause wherever you are and ask yourself: How do I *really* feel? What's coming up for me right now? And, how has that changed throughout the day (or week or month)?

You might just take a quick moment to assess, almost as if you're scanning your body for information, or you might take a moment to journal about it. You may even notice that wave of feelings, as

Dr. Tsabary described, wash over you. Or maybe it's difficult for you to discern right now how you *really* feel (your mind might be thinking, *good, I guess?*). This is our first step in slowing down and simply recognizing that our thoughts, feelings, and whatever else comes up is not the destination, but a continuous aspect of our journey.

And, no matter if your feelings are good, bad, or in between, trophies don't exist here. Now let's take this even one step further and figure out why the world makes it easier to live in the safe lane, even though we don't need to.

FIVE

Stop Living in the Safe Lane

Have you ever felt like if you took your eyes off the prize, even just for a second, you would mess up your entire life and ultimately regret it?

I'll let you all in on a funny, little secret: as a teenager, when I imagined my life in fifty years I saw myself growing old as a fit, sassy grandma who always had tennis plans and enough disposable income to take her grandchildren to the Cayman Islands just for fun (mind you—I had never picked up a tennis racket nor had I ever been to any island other than Long Island). I would daydream about the Old Me as a carefree and fun-loving woman, floating along from speaking engagement to family time to worldly travels without a care in the world. But, in order for me to achieve all this stuff I thought was necessary to be happy and successful, I saw my life adhering to a very strict timeline, one that got me to a certain place by a certain time with no room for exploring or experimenting or even taking an extra breather.

By the way, before you roll your eyes at this pipe dream of mine, you should know that I had *absolutely* no role models around me whose lives turned out like this, save something on MTV or on the cover of *Seventeen* Magazine. I was actually surrounded by quite the opposite. My family was a mish-mash of random decisions, and we always seemed to be flying by the seat of our pants. I mean, I was literally part of my parents' wedding (yes, I was barely walking, but I was there), and my three siblings weren't much more of an organized plan either. While my parents worked really, really hard to create a normal life for us, it wasn't without sacrifices. My dad was rarely at soccer games or dance recitals, as his jobs in the restaurant industry as a dishwasher-turned-server-turned-manager often took precedence. It seemed like something was always popping up out of nowhere to throw us off—a failed business endeavor, a family feud, a car that randomly broke down on the highway.

So, I wanted my life to be different. To be purposeful. To be organized and neat and fit into tiny boxes that moved in an expected way. And, if it didn't the consequences felt enormous.

But, you know what the funniest part is? I didn't realize it then, but I was scared that if I didn't think of every single potential outcome and try really, really hard to make stuff work, then I wouldn't end up where I was "supposed" to be. It might seem obvious now, but then I didn't see how out of tune I was with what *I* actually wanted. I was just organizing my life within the bounds of what was deemed "acceptable" and "successful" in the world that I was familiar with. I expected that by creating these bounds for myself, I would live a life free of fear and regret. But in reality, I was setting myself to dive into a life that simply just avoided wrong-turns, instead of driving somewhere with a purpose.

We saw in the last chapter how our generation specifically has been trained to search for happiness and "success" without actually recognizing what's right in front of our noses. To achieve and continuously move on to the Next Best Thing. To look for validation outside of ourselves. But, if we dare to dive into that a bit further, we might discover that the goals we're setting for ourselves don't consider the stuff that actually lights us up; instead, they're derived from what we're "supposed" to do.

And so, we keep chugging along like robot-humans with our eyes glued to our phones or our calendars without creating space to assess those goals, that strict way of operating, until it's too late. Until we're ninety (or fifty) and wallowing in regret. Until we realize that yes, in fact, it was probably safer to step off The Path than I imagined. And heck, maybe it was my duty to live in my intention, instead of in my parent's (or teacher's or society's). As we enter adulthood, especially in our modern world, we're conditioned to believe that the stakes are too high to experiment. To take a turn that's a bit too wide. To veer off our path.

By sticking too closely to The Path that's been laid out for us, instead of being open to the random, it sets us up for a life of regret much more than we'd expect. Take it from Jim Carey, the famous comedian and actor, after seeing his father (who could have been a famous comedian, according to Carey) get laid off from his very-boring-but-stable accounting job. Upon reflection, Carey says: "I learned many great lessons from my father, not the least of which was that you can fail at what you don't want to do so you might as well take a chance on doing what you love."

You might be able to paste that quote on your wall. Unlike our classic Reach for The Moon reminders, this one is a blaring call to wake the heck up. And, it's a message that couldn't be more relevant in our world today, when nothing *is* as it seems. But, it's still a scary concept to put into action. So, let's see why these ideas aren't just nice-to-have—but statistically, it's safer to take a risk than we might imagine.

It really, really might not feel like it at all, but the world truly is getting better

Some people might think that the idea of "doing what you love" is for Millennial snowflakes. That taking risks isn't possible in our dangerous, scary, uncertain world. Listen, I get it. We live in a fear-based place, and acting out of passion is a scary thing to do. It's risky. It takes courage. And, I also understand that it's not available to everyone at every moment. But, regardless what your mindset is about living a life of choice over negotiation, the numbers show that by society's standards the world we're operating in today is pretty damn good. I mean, yes there are a million and one things wrong (a global pandemic, climate change, growing economic divides, racial inequality that seems to be getting worse, just to name a few). But, we can take a breather for a moment. On a scale of hunter-gatherers to Uber Eats, we're collectively moving towards a lifestyle of ease, comfort, and justice.

For one, our world has been skewing toward justice for the last few decades (I know, it feels ironic to even type this sentence right now, but it's true.) Since 1996, extreme global poverty has fallen by half. *Half.* That means human beings around the world are literally starving less and have higher education rates—and that's showing up in the way we elect leaders, too. You might laugh, but political scientist Daniel Treisman recently told VOX News, "the proportion of democracies worldwide is at or near an all-time high."

And even though in 2020, the year this book was originally published, the entire globe experienced one of the deadliest health pandemics our species has seen, our human life span has more than doubled in the past two centuries. That means human beings in every corner of the world can expect to live twice as long as our ancestors, on average, and our global average life expectancy is *higher* than it was in any single country in 1950. And, since we Millennials were born? The human race has added about six years to our already-long lives. These advances for humanity aren't only due to better healthcare or technology—we've created improvements across the board, whether it's our housing, sanitation systems, and even our diet.

It's easy to think that our world is going to shit—because that's all we hear about in our modern, information-driven world. And, while I'm not at all shying away from the really terrible stuff that's happening at this moment, it's normal for us as human beings to continuously focus on the bad. Our brains are literally wired that way; negative experiences affect us more intensely than positive ones do, and for longer amounts of time. This brain structure was vital for our existence as a species during the days of getting chased by lions (literally) and when picking certain berries could kill you. But, in our modern world our brain's circuit board hasn't really adjusted yet. And it doesn't help that scary stuff, like bad economic news, tends to get covered more in news cycles, which are always on in our world today.

So, I definitely get it; I know that it feels scary to step off The Path. It seems like if we do end up taking a risk, our lives will go to shit. I felt that way, too. Even though things are statistically better for our world as a whole, it might not feel like it to you. Or me. Or anyone who gets angry when their train arrives a minute too late or they take one tiny glance at Twitter. Jia Tolentino, who is a writer for *The New Yorker* and author of the book, *Trick Mirror*, sums up this confusion perfectly: "I have become acutely conscious of the way my brain degrades when I strap it in to receive the full barrage of the internet: births, deaths, boasts, bombings, jokes, job announcements, ads, warnings, complaints, confessions, and political disasters blitzing our frayed neurons in huge waves of information that pummel us and then are instantly replaced." Jia goes on to list all of the terrible news that blitzed our frayed neurons during what was called "the worst year ever" (the list of bad things that happened in 2016 was so long that I literally couldn't include it all here for copyright reasons). But, Jia concludes this blog post for *The New Yorker*, one where she reflected on events like the Pulse nightclub shooting and The North Pole's thirty-six-degree rise in temperature with this poignant-yet-relatable concept: "And in front of this backdrop, there were all of us—our stupid selves, with our stupid frustrations, our lost baggage and delayed trains."

So, it might not come as a surprise that even though we're living in a world that's statistically skewing towards comfort and justice over the long term, our mental health right now has taken a turn for the worst. Now, more than ever, young people are reporting the highest indices of anxiety and depression that we've ever seen. From 2013 to 2016, rates of reported depression in Millennials rose nearly fifty percent. And, rates of psychological distress, such as feeling "nervous, hopeless or that everything in life takes effort" rose by 71 percent in young people aged 18 to 25. We feel less fulfilled in our jobs, in our relationships, and less sure of our future. Sadly, at least thirty percent of us Millennials see ourselves as less well-off across a variety of measures than we expected to be at that age. And, for those younger than us, like Gen Z? The predictions get worse.

But, our collective mental health as a generation is something that's in our control to change. Longevity expert and Blue Zones founder Dan Buettner has been studying trends in the longest-living, happiest, and healthiest communities around the world for over twenty years. Dan has researched the pockets of the world that have the highest number of centennials, or those who live to be one-hundred, and found a few important factors that have helped them craft a so-called *good* life.

While he says there's no magic pill, if he *could* bottle something up for all of us to live happier, more meaningful lives what do you think it would be? Purpose.

One of the key components to live a "good" life is feeling as though you have a purpose in your world, according to those who have crafted a *good* life in every single culture from islands in Japan to suburbs in California. It's not about collecting trophies to put on your shelf, or being able to change the name of your job title on LinkedIn. It's not about achieving your five-year plan perfectly. Heck, it's not even about curing cancer like your parents thought you would. It's about feeling as though you matter in this world and that the choices you make every single day matter to others, too. It's the small, regular stuff that impacts us the most.

And, most importantly living a life of purpose rather than merely avoiding regret is so much bigger than you. It quickly dissipates any worry that may begin to circle in your mind when you begin to take your eyes off The Safe Lane. Because living a purpose-driven life doesn't just take your own successes or failures into account. It indicates that your life's work means something more than the check you bring home at the end of the week, or what kind of car you drive.

Take it from Lin-Manuel Miranda, the brilliant composer and Broadway star behind musicals like *Hamilton* and *In The Heights.* Miranda, upon graduating from college, started his career as an English teacher, although he had already written and performed *In The Heights* in his college theater program. As he reflected on those early days of adulthood, his perception of the time living in The Safe Lane, he remembered the tired afternoons when he would get a glimpse of his life thirty years into his future, grading papers without having lived out his purpose. But, he said, "Something kept tapping me on the shoulder. And, I knew I couldn't *not* listen. You have to respond to things that won't leave you alone—whether that's an idea or an injustice."

In order to act from a place of purpose, of actually listening to that idea or injustice that won't leave you alone, we have to completely reorient our mindset. Throughout the next two parts of our time together in this book, we'll start to apply that thinking to your life, specifically. But, in order to get there, we first need to believe that it's okay, and actually extremely vital to our success in life, to step off The Path (if we want to), to take a risk or two, and to begin experimenting with the random.

What's the worst that could happen?

I recently had lunch with an old professor of mine from college. We'll call her Professor Carey. Back in the day, I thought she had it all—a cool job at a popular media company, a nice apartment in New York City, and a role as an adjunct professor at a prestigious university. She seemed to be living the quintessential thirty-something-year-old life as a trendy New Yorker. Most importantly, I looked up to her, because from my view it seemed like she lived a life devoid of regrets. After obtaining her law degree from an Ivy League school, she said screw it and went into journalism.

It wasn't until I had a one-on-one, unfiltered conversation with her years later that I realized she lived most of her life in the safe lane. Many times, throughout our mimosa-filled meal, she wistfully wondered, "what [my] life would be like if I stopped following the rules." She pondered out loud what she might be doing instead, if she just took that cute boy up on his study-buddy offer after 1L, or accepted a job in Austin instead of fulfilling her arbitrary mandate of how long she needed to live in New York after law school. Even though it seemed like she had everything, there was something inside of her that oozed with regret.

This conversation made me sad for many reasons—and not only because I was in the process of writing a book about exactly how *not* to become forty (or ninety) and full of regret. Mostly because these types of conversations happen all the freakin' time. They happen in bars between work colleagues and old friends on a beach vacation. They happen in nursing homes and at dinner tables and within the quietness of our own private thoughts. And, they all center around a similar question: What *was* the worst that could have happened? What was I so afraid of?

So, think about it for a moment: have you ever looked at something really scary straight in the eye and thought, *What's the worst that could happen?* Maybe it was during a trip to Costa Rica when you were triple-dog-dared to jump off a cliff into the ocean. Or maybe it was when you decided to go on a date with a seemingly nice person you met on the checkout line at Trader Joes.

Or maybe, like Professor Carey, you've been so stuck in your tunnel-vision, achievement-focused path you've never given yourself the chance.

We know that us Millennials, for a variety of reasons not within our control, have been trained to achieve and move on. We've been taught to stick to our bulleted-list of accomplishments on our résumé and venture no further. We've been conditioned to believe that it's scary and risky and potentially harmful to veer off The Path. To experiment. To shrug your shoulders and ask, "What's the worst that could happen?" As our friend Don Miguel Ruiz described ever so poetically: "We are so well trained that we are our own domesticator. We [even] punish ourselves when we don't follow the rules according to our belief system." Essentially, we are always fearing the worst—and our lives pan out accordingly.

But, we're finding that in our pretty-damn-safe world, the *worst* that could happen ain't so bad. As everything, from getting food delivered straight to your door to finding and applying for jobs from the comfort of your couch, gets infinitely easier for humans on the whole, the bar to take risks inherently gets lower. But, you know what rises? Our likelihood of feeling depressed, anxious, and regretful about the what-ifs when we're stuck living in our tunnel-vision world.

It might seem like choosing to live out of passion is inherently risky. By breaking the clear line in your résumé, you open yourself up to all what-ifs. By taking a gap year before college, we're only primed to look at what we're missing out on instead of what we're gaining. And heck, I'm not saying to go out and do all those things without deep reflection beforehand. But at the face of it, the ability to collect many random experiences, is proven to lead to much more success than we otherwise might expect. Take it from Leonard Mlodinow, a physicist, author, professor, computer game designer, *and* professional screenwriter whom we heard from in Chapter Three about unconscious behavior. He's also authored a book about how life is a lot more random than we think: "When we're in college, we think about our future as a direct line from now to then, from here to there. You might get an internship at a financial services firm, then become an assistant, and gradually move up until someday you're the boss. That's a fine life's path. But if you look at the careers of many successful people, you'll find their root is far more sinuous. And if you look at happy people, you'll find even fewer who traveled a straight line."

In either scenario, there's nothing wrong with any of the outcomes, as long as we're acting from a place of purpose rather than fear. As long as we're not afraid of what might happen if going from Here to There is less of a straight line than we may have imagined. As long as all these external markers of success aren't the only thing that's driving us towards the Next Best Thing.

When I was still on my very linear path from internship to boss at the investment bank, I teetered on the edge of stepping off The Path, too scared to actually step off. I looked around at others who took risks, who seemed like they were living these really badass (very risky) lives and could not fathom how they did it. How *does* one go about becoming a *National Geographic* photographer? An environmental designer at Patagonia? A best-selling author? A cool, young mother who was also a creative director at a startup? Their lives seemed like a random mish-mash of decisions that ended up working out for them, but a pulsing question in the back of my mind left me frozen with fear: what if it doesn't?

It wasn't until one of my best friends, my "work wife," took the leap and stepped off The Path, I woke the heck up. Talking to my friend, we'll call her Allie, via BBM (oh, the days before Slack!) was sometimes the only thing that got me through the day. We were both so dismayed by The Path from the moment we arrived in Adulthood that we connected on a deep level. So, you'll imagine my reaction when she told me that she finally took the leap, and decided to go to graduate school in Europe. It felt like a gut punch. Like a bucket of cold water was thrown over my head.

But also, it made stepping off The Path seem *so* much less risky after all. Because, when Allie explained her thought process, her "why" was so clear. She wasn't viewing this decision from a fear-based place. She was looking at it as an opportunity. She was asking herself, "What's the worst that could happen?" rather than, "What if it doesn't work out?" And, it shifted something in me. It allowed me to pick my head up and stop searching for the

Next Best Thing while simultaneously frozen with fear that life could go wrong.

I didn't make this shift overnight, though. It took many months of undoing, of reshifting, of seeing the world a tiny bit differently for me to dip a toe off The Path. After I saw Allie begin to move through her seemingly-risky-but-not-so-risky decisions with grace and courage, I started to put my feelers out there. I started to question why this job (and everything else in my life) that felt so misaligned with my purpose was holding me to them. Was it because of the financial risk that could come with leaving that investment bank? Or the reputational one—how would people know I was "smart" if they didn't see it on my résumé first?

I began to get really intentional with the choices I made—not simply just to take risks for the sake of it, but to question why I was scared of the risks in the first place. I forced myself to look deeply at the difference between those two mindset-shifting questions: "What if it doesn't work out?" versus "What's the worst that could happen?" And, I found a magical tension between the two. So much magic that it led me to take seemingly major risks—like leaving said bank to work at a small, no-name philanthropic venture fund so I could "learn" about social impact, or moving out to the West Coast with my then-boyfriend, Dupi, so we could experience a new city—that ended up driving my path to exactly where I am right now: writing this book in my cozy Brooklyn apartment with my adorable puppy and lovely fiancé, based on the blog that I built over three very seemingly risky years.

As I said, this ability to go from an obsession with life fitting in a neat box to diving head-first into risks wasn't natural for me. There were a few tactical tools that helped me shift from a fear-based to opportunity-based mindset. During the next two sections of our time together, we'll work through these in detail. But, there are two simple mindset hacks that I want to share with you right now. Often, we're taught to reach for goals, to write them down, to make them SMART, to plaster them on vision boards and across our social media profiles. But, what if we turned that idea on its head? We know where setting goals has gotten us; and if they're rooted in fear or far from our values, they ultimately set us up for failure.

One of my favorite podcast hosts, Ted Talkers, and strategically not-risky humans, Tim Ferriss, came up with this exercise after he found himself paralyzed in fear when faced with a potentially life-changing decision. In his now-viral Ted Talk on fear-setting, he walks through the importance of defining and naming our fears instead of our potential opportunities, because they often are the reason that we don't go through with a seemingly random or risky decision. Remember how our brains hold onto negative information more often than positive? Well, we're going to come back to this exercise later in the book with some specifics after we've done some deep work on ourselves, but for now, let's think about fear in a not-so-scary way.

We're simply going to get ourselves in the headspace of confronting some deep beliefs that lurk in the shadows of our mind. The second half of this book is very exercise-focused; we're going to do a lot of reflecting and analyzing. So, let's start right now by brain dumping all the fears we might have around living the life that we've always dreamed of. Start by jotting down your thoughts to the following question (remember, no judgment—brain dumps really mean you're allowing your thoughts to flow from brain to paper without censoring them):

What am I really scared of?

In this moment, right now, what does my fear look like? What is it centering on? Where do I think it comes from? If I had to give it a color or a name what would it be? If I turned my fear into a person, what would I say to them?

Now, take a pause. Doesn't that feel a bit better already? We know that the simple act of getting our feelings out of our minds and into the world gives them less importance. But oftentimes, fear creeps up on us and we don't even realize it. It lurks in corners and behind old cobwebs we've forgotten about. So, in order to address it, we need to shine a light.

Before we move on, we're going to tap into one more tool. This one is quite the opposite of the stuff we've been thinking about lately. It's all about seeing your bravery up close. It's about reconnecting to that strong, all-knowing part of you that *always* figures out what to do, even if you can't wrap your head around where that knowledge came from. It's a deep sense of courage, of strength, of bravery—in the face of fear. It's what comes after the scary stuff.

I came across this exercise during a really anxiety-ridden time, just as I was finishing the first draft of this book. It wasn't too long ago; we were in the early days of the global Coronavirus pandemic—a really, really scary experience that made all us humans around the world question our safety. Our livelihoods. It made us reconsider the level of riskiness, really, that comes with living in our modern world. It made us question, a million times a day: what if the worst does, in fact, happen to me?

As we all huddled in our houses and apartments, as we stood six feet away from each other in line at the supermarket and woke up in the middle of the night with panic attacks, we wondered how we would move through this time while facing our fears up close. I remember coming across a video by Elizabeth Gilbert, the world-renowned writer and storyteller behind books like *Eat Pray Love*. In this video, she challenged viewers to stare fear in the face. She asked her community to think about a time they were brave.

So, before we start getting honest, and diving deep into peeling back all the layers, we're going to remember how beautifully strong we are. How courageous we can truly be. I'm going to leave you a space below to journal about a time that you felt really brave. A time when you did something that your mind never thought you were capable of. A time when you figured shit out even though it seemed impossible. And hey, this reminder doesn't need to be anything drastic, like climbing a mountain or saving a person from a burning building. It could be the time that you told your best friend he or she did something that bothered you. It could be allowing yourself to have a good cry, finally, all alone in your room. It could be standing up for yourself in a meeting at work or during an argument with your significant other. Bravery happens every day, every moment—every time you allow your inner-knowing to take precedent over your Baby Brain.

Remind yourself of a time when you were brave and your inner knowing overrode your mind

Now that you understand how you got Here—a place filled with trick mirrors, stories, and lies and trophies, a place where you feel like you need to constantly be happier—we can begin to *really* undo all the layers. We can figure out, together, what makes you light up, how you can live a life with *all* the feels while still paying your bills on time.

We're going to make Adulthood a choice, rather than a negotiation, starting now.

Part Three:

It's Your Life, Dammit

To free us from the expectations of others, to give us back to ourselves-there lies the great, the singular power of self-respect.

-Joan Didion

SIX

It Starts with Telling the Truth

Have you ever smiled when you really feel like shit?

It could be in line at the supermarket when the person behind you accidentally hits your ankles with their cart for the fifth time. Or maybe it's when your boss asks if you could make *just one more* round of edits to the presentation due tomorrow, even though you've been doing exactly what he or she passive-aggressively suggests all week. Or maybe it's when you groan, "I'm *fiiine*" to your mom over the phone, as you stuff a day-old burrito into your mouth and stare at your half-dead plants from the comfort of your twin bed.

Not that I'm projecting *anything* onto you with these examples, but surely there have been times in your life where you've found yourself sacrificing how you *really* feel for the sake of making others comfortable. For the sake of not causing a ruckus. For the sake of making it seem to your boss, or your mom, or strangers—or even yourself—that everything is just fine. This is the way life is supposed to be, we believe, so we shrug our shoulders, push down our frustrations, and paste on a smile.

If this question feels like it's igniting something deep inside of you, that's good. If it feels like a hazy dream, like "Oh yeah, maybe there was a time when I pretended . . . " that's great. We're starting to wake the heck up. We're beginning to see that hey, maybe a lot of this confusing stuff I'm feeling is normal. It's stuff I've been trained to do, to believe, to act on for my entire life so far—and although it wasn't anyone's malicious doing, it shaped my entire world view. Now, it's time to stare that training in the face. It's time to start telling the truth about what the hell we want out of life and actually do something about it.

Because, listen: We all tell lies, all the time—to people close to us, mere strangers, and sadly, to ourselves. In a way, our world today forces us to do so. We're all so seemingly busy and distracted, that it feels like we don't have *time* to assess how we really feel—let alone share it. We're constantly running on the work-gym-sleep hamster wheel of life, looking toward that Next Shiny Thing, so we slap on a smile in order to keep trudging along. Then, when we *do* actually have time to pause, we find ways to incessantly distract ourselves. It could be hours spent scrolling through Facebook, or mindlessly watching an entire season of *The Office* without moving from your couch. It could be the need to have *just one* glass of wine to wind down from a day at work—that turns into the bottle (hey—no judgment here; I totally am the one who eats burritos from bed). Or it could simply be never actually leaving work and answering emails from bed until midnight.

Regardless if we have time or not (we do), our world acts like feeling your feelings and then talking about them is the end of your life as a successful human being. Think about all the mantras we've been taught throughout our childhood: "Mind over matter," "Get over it," or "Suck it up" are all common ones that imply feeling or crying or releasing emotion is looked down upon.

How many times have you been warned that if you cry during a difficult work meeting, you're essentially committing career "suicide" (which is all so, so wrong in so many ways, but you know you've thought twice before doing it)? Character qualities, like stoicism and strength, have been prized since long before any of us reading this book were born. I mean, it's partially biological—back in the days of early human evolution, researchers have found that the original smile was an act rooted in fear. Though nowadays we associate smiles with joy and happiness, smiling—or bearing our teeth—was used as a submissive act in order to diffuse aggression. Even then, we were hiding how we really felt. You can thank your ancient ancestors for the awkward, toothy grin that spreads across your face when a sweaty person on the subway bumps into you for the tenth time, even though anger is rising in your chest.

But today, we're not often in true danger when we mask our emotions with pseudo-happiness. You can think of your feelings, no matter how deep or fleeting they are, as clues to what you really want. They are like little puzzle pieces that guide us toward creating a life of choice, rather than negotiation. So, feeling our feelings instead of pushing them away is the first step towards crafting a life of passion, purpose, and pure joy (truly). And, most importantly—it's a vital aspect of living a life that's happy, healthy, and lengthy. The latest neuroscience research is now finding that when an emotion, which is a hard-wired biological response to an experience, arises in our bodies and we ignore it, our bodies get creative. They take this energy and store it in our physical bodies and our brains as stress (remember our friend the Baby Brain?). And, stress from blocked emotions has been linked to both physical and mental illnesses, like heart disease, intestinal problems, and autoimmune disorders, among others.

So, getting in touch with our feelings isn't just a nice thing to do. It's vital if we want to live a long, healthy life. As we've seen in our work together so far, living in avoidance and persevering through the tough stuff without acknowledging how we really feel is pretty much always at the root of why we tend to be "going through it" when we reach Adulthood. We get here and keep reaching for our goals, collecting all the trophies, and simultaneously pushing away the truth. We sulk over the idea that we can't "find our passion," but we keep showing up to our mediocre job, *hoping* things will be different. We get overwhelmed by bills and loans so we avoid looking at our bank statement until it's too late.

Now, I'm not here to place blame; I definitely suffered from this way of thinking, too. Because, as we've also seen, the way we react to life isn't *fully* our fault. We haven't necessarily been given the tools to process how we feel and make sense of all that messy truth before. So, what do we do instead? We push them down. Look for distractions. Bat away tears of frustration for the sake of others. Pretend everything is "fine" and move on. Power through the tough stuff until we reach our shiny goal.

The rest of this book is going to be confronting the tough stuff. It's going to be looking that truth straight in the eye and making sense of it all. It's going to be collecting the tools so that yes, you can feel like shit and actually acknowledge it. This is the turning point of our time together so far, because now we're *doing the work* (if you think we've already done that, damn, you're in for a treat). From this point forward, we're going to be reflecting and thinking and diving deep. We're going to ask ourselves questions we've likely never thought about before; work through exercises and journaling prompts that might feel foreign; and get really, really honest about our feelings.

Now it's my turn to be completely honest: this is going to be hard and weird at first. I know, because I've done every single one of these exercises myself (many, many times) and with hundreds of humans like us, too. And, I know that it's awkward and scary to pull back those curtains on stuff you thought you could avoid forever. These types of exercises force us to look all of our trick mirrors in the eye and see through that gross haze from the Carnival smoke machine.

If it helps, you can think of me as your (slightly) older sister who's in her sophomore year of college while you're in the midst of applications. I'm right on the other side of it all—and I remember so clearly how confusing it was to navigate. How I felt like my insides were being tangled every time someone asked, "So, how are you?" I obviously couldn't tell them the truth, so I pushed those feelings aside. And, my purpose here is to hold space for you to actually . . . feel them.

So, no matter where you are in this process of *doing the work*, whether you're lying on a beach pretending that email doesn't exist or slightly sobbing late at night in your bed, I've been there. And, we're going to go through it together. Take this at your own pace, in your own time, doing it your own way. I've worked with so many different types of humans on this kind of stuff, and from my experience, everyone works differently. Some of us have more layers to peel back than others; some have more resistance to those layers than others. The most important thing, as we've seen, is to simply start by telling the truth. And remember, you don't need to share this truth with anyone, except You. You don't need to broadcast these reflections out into the ether (unless you want to). The next few chapters of truth-telling are for you and you only—until (if ever) you're ready to share.

So, let's start peeling back the layers.

The truth comes out when you're alone

Being alone is underrated. In a world of FOMO (Fear Of Missing Out, for you old folks), it can feel like we have to be doing something with other people at all times. But, being alone is the first place that we begin to connect with our feelings. It's the space where we start to tell the truth.

Growing up in a loud, chaotic house with three younger siblings, I barely knew what "alone time" meant. Actually, when I got to college I realized that it was *weird* that I wasn't fazed by the blaring horns outside of my dorm window. My roommates, who had all come from quiet, poised families in wealthy zip codes, couldn't sleep in our bedroom in the center of New York City's Union Square. I, on the other hand, thrived in the chaos. The louder, the better (I thought). What I didn't realize was that filling my calendar with busyness, and filling my mind with noise helped me avoid getting to know myself. It forced me to push away my feelings, my truths, because I was so distracted by everything else.

So, the first time that I truly spent time alone in my *entire life* (seriously) was when I was twenty-one. Well, you already know that I spent months in the South Pacific by my lonesome, a radical task for someone whose parents would bring homemade dinner in Tupperware dishes to her college dorm each week. But, twenty-one-year-old me dove into this new experience head-first. My over-achiever personality shone through *real* clear (oh, how I cringe looking back at those early days). It's honestly pretty hysterical reflecting on it now; I literally planned my four-month trip out by the day in a tiny Moleskin notebook. That's 121 individual plans scribbled down and researched before I even stepped foot in the country. I thought that the only way to cope, to have *fun* was to keep myself busy for every moment of every day. I made plans with people I didn't even know the name of; I said yes to every invitation (like, say, getting into a van with strangers to find a secret waterfall and jump off the top of it, even though every fiber of my being was scared shitless); I convinced myself that the whole *point* of this all was to make friends and do crazy stuff. To get it out of my system before Real Life began. So, I made sure that I barely had any time to think. I was running away from my feelings so quickly, I didn't even realize they were there.

It wasn't until a long, overnight bus ride about halfway through my trip that I started to get an inkling that I was doing it all wrong. I had never really considered that this period of extended travel was about spending time with myself, not just exploring the world and making friends. I was never before encouraged to simply be—to live fully in the present moment and see what comes. To stop scheduling and planning and overcommitting for the sake of deciding what *feels good* in that moment. It's an underrated skill that is so far out of the context of our modern world that I didn't even know it existed.

We'll call my seatmate Greta, a German girl who was also twenty-one and an early college grad, but way more mature and way less anxious than I. As we settled into our uncomfortable Greyhound seats and prepared for the night, Greta must have noticed me scouring my notebook for the next plans. She looked over and asked, "Surfer's Paradise, too? Do you know where you're staying yet? I haven't booked a hostel, but I heard Down Under is good." I looked up from my encyclopedia-like book in sheer horror. My face must have mirrored my thoughts, because Greta let out a snort-laugh and said, "Okay, looks like I'm staying where you're staying, Miss Organized." Leave it to Germans and their wry sense of humor, huh?

Although we didn't necessarily start out as best friends, and the fact that we only really connected for twenty-four hours at most, Greta ended up becoming one of the most impactful humans I interacted with on that trip, and maybe even in my life. I weirdly think about her often, though we didn't even become Facebook friends. She was the first person who ever probed (and consequently gave me the permission I was seeking) as to why I was trying so hard. She questioned why I was running away from the whirlwind of feelings that was circling around me instead of facing them head-on. And most importantly, Greta, a twenty-one-year-old girl from a small town in Germany, gave me the best piece of advice I've yet to receive. On a casual walk the next morning through Surfer's Paradise, a Jersey Shore-esque beach town in Australia, Greta (who was still utterly confused by my need to collect metaphorical trophies, even on "vacation") shrugged her shoulders and said: "Katina—not everything you do needs to have a bigger purpose. It doesn't all need to add up to something. Sometimes, you need to just live a little, sit on the beach, and enjoy. You Americans are funny. I bet you'll look back on this trip and think, *Wow, this really changed my life*. And, you were doing nothing, on a beach, all by yourself."

Greta couldn't have known how much her words would, in fact, change the course of my life. Because, after she said that, I couldn't unsee my eagerness to make this trip *mean* something. Every time I was alone, my brain would start to churn. My to-do lists would run like a hamster wheel in my brain. I would question: Is this a productive use of my time? I felt like I needed to squeeze the living daylight out of every moment, so I could tell all my friends and family and co-workers that it was worth it. To ensure that my precious time spent floating around the South Pacific instead of working and optimizing and getting ahead actually mattered. I was so fixated on making sure that every moment fully counted, I was always jumping into the Next Best Thing. The next place I was going, thing I was doing, person I was meeting. And, I totally missed the point.

So, thanks to Greta's sage advice, I loosened the reigns a bit and actually started spending time alone. I traveled up to Brisbane next and made a (very intense, I know that's clearly a theme here) commitment not to speak a single word to anyone. I wanted to take a breather, to sit, to journal, to think. To lay in the park and literally not do anything. How many times had I ever done that—without worrying in the back of my mind that I *should* be doing something else? Or how weird I was? Or what other people would think?

This skill, one of consciously spending time by yourself, started off rocky for me. The first few times I did it, I tried to find nearly any distraction or excuse to stop myself. Because, once you break the barrier, it seems like an avalanche of thoughts and feelings come barreling toward you. We've seen how normal it is to lie to ourselves and push those feelings away. But, I did something different after my conversation with Greta. I started to get those feelings out of my body and my head—and into the world. I wrote them down. I allowed them to flow through me and out of me. I stopped holding onto them or pushing them away and simply acknowledged them.

Only a few days after meeting Greta, it was Valentine's Day. Now, normally Valentine's Day wasn't a "terrible" holiday according to my Baby Brain; I had the same boyfriend throughout pretty much of all high school and college (boring, I know), so it became almost a non-holiday for me at that point. But, 2014 was different. I had broken up with said boyfriend after many attempts (it was always me doing the breaking up *and* the returning), right before leaving for Australia. So, I was pretty raw. My normal self would have pushed my feelings of sadness and confusion away by doing *literally* anything else—pretending they don't exist, going out and forgetting about them, acting like I didn't care. But, Greta inspired me to think a bit differently.

So, I sat outside of my janky hostel watching couples canoodle and kiss and roll around on the beach. And, I felt tears begin to well behind my eyes. They stung, and at first, it felt like something really terrible was happening, I hadn't allowed myself to cry in so long, I kind of forgot what it felt like. But, after a few moments I was full-blown sobbing. I'm not shitting you—I sat on a bench with a bar of Cadbury chocolate and cried. All by myself. On Valentine's Day. It seemed like it could have been a scene out of a really bad Rom Com. But, you know what? That release felt so insanely good, like I had been holding up a well for decades and it was finally letting go, I honestly never looked back.

You might be sitting here thinking: *Wow, great for you Katina but that's literally impossible for me. Also, who sits outside and cries by themselves? I'm not going to Australia. I don't have a Greta in my life. You're also so, so weird . . .* The list can go on—but, just take a moment right now and notice all the resistance and excuses that are beginning to arise for you. What feels weird about spending time alone? Or allowing your feelings to flow? Would you do it? Have you ever? Take a couple of moments and check in with what's coming up for you right now.

This ability to be your own best friend, your own mentor, your own everything, really, is the first step in any of the work we're going to do together. It's a necessary foundation in order to assess and check in with yourself. And, while spending time alone while you're running errands or in a workout class is great, there's a slight difference between being alone and being *alone*. You catch my drift? Sometimes we're alone, but running through our mental to-do list and not consciously there. When I say spend time alone, I really mean it. Act like you're going to catch up with an old friend, but it's really You. You're allowing your Inner Knowing to shine through, and quiet your Baby Brain once and for all.

If you're racking your brain for ways that you can consciously spend time by yourself, here are some of my favorite ways to get started. One of my favorite authors, Julia Cameron, is an OG in the world of self-reflection. She calls this time alone "Inspiration Dates"—a concept I've always loved. We know that the idea of spending time alone can be intimidating, so if we shift our mindset just a bit to think that it's actually a special treat, it makes it even more exciting. These are some of my favorite Inspiration Dates to take myself on:

- Go for a walk or run sans distraction, without scrolling through your phone or listening to a podcast
- Spend some time journaling. My favorite example of this is the "Brain Dump" or Morning Pages exercise (also by Julia Cameron). Simply, write without judgment or distractions right when you wake up for five to ten minutes. There doesn't need to be a purpose; the only purpose is to release your thoughts.
- Start a meditation practice (or sitting-in-silence-for-5-minutes-with-your-coffee practice). We'll talk more about this in Part Four.

Being proactive about this practice of spending time alone is key. So, start scheduling time into your calendar, just as you would a happy hour with friends (this time, your date is with your best friend, You, remember?). Trust me, you'll want to avoid it at first. But, the more often you can show up for yourself, the easier it gets.

Before we dive into some reflection work, let's make a commitment to actively spend time by yourself in the coming days and weeks (heck, years!). I find that by writing down a promise to yourself, it helps it stick (and science backs this up, too). I'm your accountability buddy—so, tell me, when and how often will you spend time actively with You in the near future?

Take off your rose-colored (or poop-colored) glasses

We already know how normal it is to move through life unconsciously on that work-gym-sleep hamster wheel, letting our big ol' Baby Brains take charge. But, how do we shift into that awareness? How do we begin to actually feel those feelings without resistance?

One of my favorite exercises that helps me tap into this way of thinking is to assess our lives Right Now. Seriously. I know, it's probably the last thing you want to do—something you've been avoiding thinking about in every way possible. But we're not going to hold back any longer. We're going to peel back the layers, look at the good stuff, the tough stuff, the ugly stuff, and get real for a moment. This is our first step in telling the truth.

You've already committed to a practice of spending more time getting to know yourself, but in order to walk into that meeting with You most prepared, let's do some thinking and reflecting together. Part of what I do through On Adulting is work one-on-one with hundreds of humans (just like you!) who are confused about their lives. They don't know what their passion is, how to create a life that they love while also paying the bills, and honestly, where they would even start. So, we're going to wrap up this chapter in truth telling by completing my favorite, and first, exercise I do with my coaching clients. We're going to assess your life Right Now.

Get out a pen and paper, or again, use the space in this book. If you're not feeling ready to do a little thinking and reflecting right now that's also cool. I one-hundred percent believe that reflection shouldn't be forced, so make sure that you complete this exercise when you have the time and headspace to dive into it fully. You might read through this to preview what we'll do and come back to it when you're not on the subway or half-asleep or whatever.

I'm going to lay out a bunch of different areas of your life below, and you'll answer a few questions about them. Remember, there's literally nothing for you to hide here. No one else will see this book, unless you want to share it. You don't need to broadcast this on Instagram or blab about it to your best friend. This is for your eyes only. Think of it as your elementary school diary with a lock on the outside; your mom or siblings won't be peaking in. So, be real. Be honest. Tell the absolute truth, because that's the only way we're going to make progress.

Below, you'll see that there are eight different areas of your life. Rate them on a scale of one (being, this is so insanely terrible that I can't bear to think about it) to ten (being, this is so freakin' amazing that I feel like I'm floating on a cloud whenever I experience it). There are a few questions to consider and further reflect on as well; you may dive into these at a later time or use them to go deeper in asking why. Our purpose with this exercise is to create a starting point, to begin telling the truth, about all the areas of your life so we can begin to make progress where it's needed. Remember: we're not looking forward just yet. There's no need to make plans or analyze how to make stuff better. We are simply going to practice being in the moment, and stare your life in the face as it is currently.

Here we go:

Aspect of Life	Questions to consider	Rating (1 - 10)
General well-being	How do you feel on a day-to-day basis? Do you walk through life feeling narrow + stuck or expansive + free?	
Career & purpose	What does your job feel like Right Now? Do you look up to people around you and feel like you're learning from them? Are you feeling challenged and fulfilled? Do you have a vision of what your ultimate purpose is? Are you working toward making that a reality, in any way?	
Romantic relationships & self-love	Do you feel comfortable being alone with just You? Do you feel like you know who you are enough—that you could begin to share love with others? How important is it for you to connect deeply with another human—and are you doing it right now?	

Aspect of Life	Questions to consider	Rating (1 - 10)
Family & friend relationships	Do you have a group of humans—blood-related or otherwise—that you can rely on? Do you think you have clear boundaries with them?	
Financial health	If you were to look at your bank account right now, how would you feel? Do you feel like money is always scarce or abundant? Do you feel like you'll be paying loans for the rest of your life—or you have the potential to be completely debt-free? Do you feel comfortable accepting gifts (or even a cup of coffee) from someone without feeling bad about it?	
Physical health	Are you caring for yourself from the inside out? Are you able to move your body consistently in a way that feels good for you? Do you have an unrealistic perception of how you should look? Does your physical health consume your mind, or is it simply just one aspect of your general well-being?	
Home & daily living	How does your home environment feel? Does it bring you joy and a sense of groundedness or more like stress and worry? Do you feel like you have time and space for all the stuff you want to do in your everyday life?	

Aspect of Life	Questions to consider	Rating (1 - 10)
Creative well-being and sense of adventure	Do you feel like you have consistent creative hobbies that help you feel fulfilled – or you spend your "free" time scrolling? Do you create space for exploration and adventure in your everyday – or find ways to escape your life?	

Phew! That was a lot. Most of us probably haven't looked that hard at our lives as they are without planning and plotting and criticizing in a long while. Now, take a moment to think about one more thing: as you went through this exercise, how did you actually feel while doing it? Were you stuck in constant comparison mode—with yourself and everyone on your Instagram feed? Did you continue jumping ahead to how you could fix or solve it? Did you lie (gasp!) to make something seem better than it really is?

Whatever experience you had during this reflection process is a-okay. Shifting our mindsets, our entire way of looking at the world, takes a long while. For most of us, we've never *really* done it. It's a brand-new skill, a tiny muscle that we're starting to exercise. And, it's nothing like we're used to—it's not something we could check off a to-do list and feel accomplished about (no trophy-collecting here). So, if you're feeling resistance or a bit unsettled that's completely normal.

Also, if you're feeling like we haven't been able to tie a neat little bow around your reflection, you're right. We're taking each aspect of this process step-by-step, and we won't come out with clear black-and-white answers in this exact moment (or heck, maybe ever). Each exercise we do, especially this tool we worked through, is something you can return to many, many times over the course of your life. It's meant to be a conduit for a reflection and check-in practice that you build into your lifestyle over the long-term. So, think of this exercise as a guide, a starting point really. You may add or subtract certain portions of it depending on what you need. Imagine what we're doing right now as reflection-with-training-wheels, and soon you'll be riding into the distance all by your lonesome.

But, for now, we're going to keep doing it together.

SEVEN

You Won't Get in Trouble for Daydreaming Here

Do you feel like your dreams aren't realistic and you'll never figure out your "passion"?

I mean, fuck being realistic, right? That's the issue that got us here in the first place. We tried to follow the rules, stay on The Path, become emergency room doctors instead of writers and look where it got us. It got us to a place where we're twenty-five and anxious, in debt, and still having to do laundry at our parents' house for crying out loud. I know I'm generalizing here, but you catch my drift. Leading a life that's realistic and logical leaves us taking regret to the grave.

For as long as I could remember, I've had one hand in the clouds and one foot on the ground. I'd often get in trouble for thinking too big, for being *unrealistic*, for batting a little too far out of my box. But, in order for the world to shake me out of my daydream I'd hear: "Katina, in the *real world*, life doesn't work that way. Life is difficult. You have to work really, really hard to make your dreams a reality. That probably won't happen." Those lessons my Baby Brain absorbed came from everywhere—teachers, my family, and even TV shows.

One experience as a kid really stuck with me, and my Baby Brain, for that matter. Back in middle school, I was a pretty chatty and outgoing kid who *also* loved science and math. On the other hand, I strongly disliked home economics to an *extreme* degree. To this day, cooking is not my thing (thankfully I'm engaged to a guy who loves it). After a particularly engaging chemistry lesson, I trotted into my home economics class and announced to anyone who would listen: "I just *love* chemistry! I think I'm going to be a chemist one day. Maybe I'll go to Harvard and study chemistry." I remember how much the excitement at the potential of this opportunity seized my little eleven-year old body. Chemistry! Harvard! The world was my oyster! Although looking back on it now, those dreams were quite unrealistic, if I'm being honest, although then I was convinced they were well within my reach. But no, my punctual, realistic home economics teacher proceeded to announce to the class: "Katina—sit down. You're too talkative to become a chemist and no one from our school goes to Harvard anyway, so that's *out of the question.*" Even though her comment angered me in the moment (and my mom very much so after school), my Baby Brain latched onto that lesson without me even realizing it. Chemistry became just another subject in school; it lost its magic. Even though my natural state was to see the world as it could be, not as it is, just by living in this world I came to believe that my dreams were impossible.

By the way, I'm not unique. Every single human being is inherently creative and idealistic—that's actually one of the main characteristics that sets us apart from our relatives in the animal kingdom. Our ability to see potential in the mundane is what makes us human over, say, a mockingbird. Our brains are hardwired to combat routine, which as neuroscientist, author, and brain behind *The Creative Brain* on Netflix David Eagleman says, "is a biological mandate. A wild imagination has characterized the history of our species. . . . It's not something only a few people do. The innovative drive lives in every human brain, and the resulting war against the repetitive is what powers the colossal changes that distinguish one generation from the next, one decade from the next, one year from the next."

So, if this is the case, why do most of us feel like we're running on a never-ending hamster wheel? Why does it feel like every year (or every day) is exactly the same, and it's so hard to create a life for ourselves filled with passion, purpose, and excitement? Over 75 percent of people today say that they don't feel like they reach their creative potential once they enter adulthood. I mean, think about your answers to that reflection exercise from last chapter—on average, do you feel like you're living up to your greatest potential? If your answer is a resounding no, well heck, you're not alone. In our world filled with knowledge-workers and speed-typers and email-checkers, we're like little lab rats (or hamsters) running from one task to the next—achieving and plotting and planning but never fulfilling. It's not that we're incapable of dreaming—it's a basic human characteristic—but that we're told our dreams are impossible so many times they become so. This isn't unique to our generation either; it's another human trait otherwise known as Status Quo Bias, which prefers things just as they are. Often, change is scary for most people, so they try to convince you not to do it.

Well, we're going to practice dreaming big, together. We're going to pretend that "rules" don't exist and experiment with what *could* happen, instead of what we *should* do next. We're going to get out of our little boxes that we've created for ourselves, with the help of all the other realistic humans around us, and see what's possible. See, I told you this chapter would be more fun, right? As the quintessential dreamer Walt Disney, once said: "First, think. Second, dream. Third, believe. And finally, dare."

Let's start dreamin'.

Break out those Milky Pens

It feels like the idea of "finding your passion" is floating around everywhere these days. I, myself, am guilty of succumbing to these messages (and even sharing them.) For a long time, I was convinced that in order to figure out your passion, your purpose for being on this Big Earth, you had to go through a magical process. In my mind, I imagined that finding your passion happened like the Sorting Hat in Harry Potter—some all-knowing being would plop down into, or on top of, my head and exclaim: "Here it is! Your passion is [fill in the blank], and it's always destined to be that way! Now, go fulfill it!" Do you catch my drift? I'm being a bit dramatic here, but nearly every Millennial I talk to, whether I'm coaching them to "find" *It* or simply just having wine and catching up with some friends, is confused. It's like we're walking around blindfolded, moving through the motions of life, and expecting to come across a neon sign that blares: PASSION FOUND HERE.

I hate to be the one to break it to you, but that is *definitely* not how it works. And, I'm not being a grouchy, old person who is discouraging you from going after your dreams. I'm speaking from a place of recent experience. Because I, too, was searching and searching for that damn thing I was supposed to do; I was constantly looking outside of myself for something, anything that meant I didn't need to stare at computer screens all day crunching numbers and wishing I was somewhere else. What I didn't realize until much later was that this whole "passion" thing has been sitting inside of me for my entire life. And, that's true for every single one of us. We just build up the layers and eventually stop listening.

In order to *find* (or remember) our purpose, we're going to start by looking backwards. We're going to take a little trip down Memory Lane and jog our brains for all the stuff we used to love doing, before we were told it was unrealistic. We're going to make some connections between, say, the imaginary games you loved to play and the way you used to boss around your younger siblings (ring a bell?) to your life right now. We're going to do some major reflecting in order to pull out those big, passionate, exciting ideas so that we can craft a version of Adulthood that makes you feel most alive.

Some of you might be thinking this all sounds impossible, that I'm the Sorting Hat now. That's okay—dreaming big can be scary. It can be (and usually is) really uncomfortable. We're taught to color in the lines for so freakin' long that when we start to dribble outside of them, we freeze. We repeat the stories that our parents and teachers and those so-called adults have told us for our entire lives: Follow the rules. Use your inside voice. Stay on The Path. But, this chapter, more than anything you've read in this book so far, is the most important one in helping you let go of those rules. We're going to journey into a world unknown, one where bills and laundry and student loans don't matter (we'll figure out how to work those in later, I promise). So, pretend for a few minutes with me and dream big. Suspend reality for a little while and I promise, we'll dive back into it soon.

It's journaling time again. Whatever process you've been using to reflect so far, keep it up (journal, spare napkin in your pocket, pretending you're doing work at your desk but making a master Google Doc of reflections instead). We have three different exercises to think through for the rest of this chapter all around dreaming big, so close your eyes for a moment, take a deep breath, and let go of reality.

First thing's first: we're going back to life as a kid. I'm going to lay out a series of questions that you can reflect on, journal about, and write out very specific answers to right now. These questions, paired with your baseline assessment of your Life Right Now (from last chapter) will be clues to understand what we need to incorporate into your life. So, take some time to think about the following ideas:

1. Let's go back to who you were around age eight. What was your personality like?

   - Did you feel more energized around a lot of people or in your own head (or both)? Did you love school or look for ways to escape? Did you feel motivated by external stuff or did you march to the beat of your own drum?

2. How did you enjoy spending your free time back then?

   - Was it painting or writing or watching TV? Was it playing sports or helping your parents manage their store? Was it trading Pokémon cards (guilty) or setting up lemonade stands? Was it all of the above or none?

3. Let's dive deeper into your free time-assess which *parts* of your free time activities were most enjoyable to you.

- Example 1: Did you love watching TV because you would repeat every line of your favorite show word-for-word after? Or did you love it for the solace of being alone and absorbed in a story? Were you instead taken by the costumes and design of the set?

- Example 2: Did you love playing soccer because you got to set a goal (score as many goals as possible) and achieve it to an insane degree? Did you love motivating your teammates and keeping morale up? Did you enjoy moving your body and understanding the mechanics of how it worked?

4. Did any of those free-time activities sneak in there that maybe you *didn't* love but thought you did? Why or why not?

- Maybe you thought you loved playing soccer but realized that you only "liked" it because your dad played in college. Maybe you didn't like anything about it at all; you actually resented going but convinced yourself otherwise.

- How does it feel to recognize that-and let it go?

I know that going through this exercise might feel a bit like you're riding your Razor Scooter for the first time in years; it feels a bit rusty and wobbly at first. I mean, when was the last time you thought about your childhood or heck, stuff you like to do for fun?

When I came up with this reflection exercise, the word *fun* wasn't something that had entered my brain in a while. I was in a place of complete and utter desperation. I had been angrily jotting away on my subway commute early one morning as I made my way into work for a seven o'clock meeting. There were a handful of other early risers on the train, and whenever we made eye contact, we'd glance at each other knowingly with a shared knowing that none of this way of living was our choice. It was probably a few months after that first reflection exercise I did in the auditorium of my mentee's high school (the one where I realized how much I loved wearing pants and being in nature, remember?). I was in a place of frustration, anger, and disappointment. This was not how I imagined my life to be turning out, I wrote. And, while I knew I was lucky to be heading to a job, I couldn't help but entertain my sadness about where I ended up. As I continued to brain dump all my frustrations, I began to see more and more clearly how out of alignment I was with my real, true self.

Because, you see—up until that point, I knew that I was desperately unhappy and confused, but I didn't know how to fix it. I was showing up to work every day with a deep (*deep*, let me tell you) understanding of how much I disliked churning out Excel models and running to the printer and sitting behind three computer screens for hours on end without a real conversation to be had—but I didn't know *what* I actually liked. I kept waiting for it to show up somewhere. I was taking the backseat in my life, because I was completely and utterly lost. I was waiting for that neon PASSION FOUND HERE sign to show up. The first time I ever really thought about what was important to me, what my life values were, was on the floor of that high school auditorium. So, dreaming about my life's purpose? That was way too far out of my realm of possibility. I was just waiting for the Sorting Hat to bestow my purpose upon me.

During that angry pre-dawn commute, I hit a breaking point. I was tired of my own bullshit. I was overwriting about my frustrations. I was ready to begin looking inside for the answers in here, instead of out *there* for validation. So, I did the simplest thing I could think of: I went back to the earliest memories of joy and fun and excitement I could conjure up, and I asked myself what I actually liked about those moments. I wasn't just *saying* I liked playing soccer or bossing around my siblings while making home videos; I was asking myself why. I was removing a layer and getting creative about the parts of my life that were missing. I completed that same exact exercise you just did, and it was almost like a magical spell was broken. Because, when I took a step back and let myself feel and dream and remember for a moment, I realized that the stuff I had always really enjoyed, but got lost somewhere along the way was writing, motivating others, and thinking about big life questions. Very causal stuff, I know.

But, when I reviewed my daily routine at the time, I was doing none of those things, not even in my so-called "free" time. My life consisted of the following: wake up, work out, churn through Excel analyses, go home and drink wine to forget about my day (seriously). On the weekends, instead of incorporating some writing or reading or connecting into my life, I committed to the typical New York way of handling stress: going to brunch with friends, napping, and getting ready to go out—until I couldn't delay real life any longer. It wasn't until that moment on the subway that I realized I didn't need to wait until my passion fell from the sky to start incorporating the stuff that brought me joy into my life. I saw that I could start writing before bed instead of dozing off to the sound of Netflix playing in the background. I could create my own community of people who were looking to talk about these big life questions instead of forgetting about their problems at a bar. I could take baby steps to begin shifting how I spent my free time right now, instead of feeling like it was all or nothing—that things could get incrementally better if I just made slight changes to my every day. I could start listening to that incessant tapping on my shoulder, as Lin-Manuel Miranda described.

Now, while this was all well and good, it didn't solve the big problem that was still nagging at me and I'm sure all of you: what was I *passionate* about? What direction was I going to head in with my life writ large? How was I going to get myself out of this soul-sucking job and to a place where I actually *enjoyed* waking up every day? How was I going to step into my purpose, one that not only impacted me but my community as well?

You might be asking yourself the same questions right now. While yes, you might love reciting *Mean Girls* in its entirety, does that mean your life path is to become an actor? Or maybe during this mind-bending exercise you remember how much you loved baking cupcakes—does that mean you should start your own cupcake company? Well, even though our generation tends toward turning our hobbies into side hustles, that isn't always the answer. Our life's purpose isn't simply a replica of what love to do in our free time. And, most importantly—it isn't only related to what we do professionally. So, knowing that, let's take our reflections up a notch.

Your North Star: the compass for the rest of your life

Everything started to come together for me when I connected to my North Star. What is a North Star, you might ask? Well, you can think of it as a personal mission statement so that we know if we are (or are not) in line with what we're meant to do. It's a holistic-but-simple way to organize your approach to life. And, we're going to establish our own North Star right now. We're going to get curious about our life purpose, our deep passions, and how the heck we can keep showing up in this world in a meaningful way.

This exercise is by far one of my favorites because it's literally life-changing. I (still) use my North Star as a guidepost for every single decision that I make—whether it's minor, like choosing to work with a client, or major, like choosing to move across the country. It's also a tool that I've seen have the biggest impact on any human that I work with, because once you're able to drive toward a bigger purpose, everything else becomes clear.

You can think of your North Star as a company would a "mission statement"—it's a one(ish) sentence description of your values and direction. As Patagonia (the company, not the place) says, it's your Reason for Being. It's why you do what you do. It's that big-picture dream that you're driving toward through every interaction you have, every job you take, and every opportunity you say yes or no to.

Every time I think about how much of a game-changer having a personal North Star statement is, I can't believe that we've never been taught to think about it before. Remember in middle school when we're given that test to determine if we'd make a better guidance counselor or mathematician? Well, in my ideal world we'd be asked to use our critical thinking skills, get in touch with our feelings, and write out our North Star. It would make so many things in life—like deciding what colleges to apply to (if we even want to go!) or what place to experiment living in—so much more fruitful.

Since we can't go back in time, let's turn the wheels forward and come up with our North Star right now. You've already been accessing this way of thinking for a few chapters now, so we're going to tie some stuff together. I know how daunting this exercise can feel (I'm creating my life purpose! The guardrails for the rest of my life!), so I'm going to share a few examples—of my own and those of some of my clients, with their permission—as well as a formula for you to come up with your own. Feel free to take as much creative reign on this as you'd like. The purpose of this exercise is for you to be able to use this statement as a *decision processing tool* as you work toward creating a life that you've always dreamed of. It should be general enough that it can shift and grow with you as you shift and grow, but specific enough that you have some direction when you're faced with a choice.

I came up with my North Star after a conversation with a longtime mentor when I was completely unsure of my *purpose*. We'll call him Luke. He is a corporate social responsibility guru who was leading Nike's social impact work at the time, and I looked up to him immensely. I knew that I was craving some type of work that made a positive impact on the world and stuff to do in my free time that nourished my creative curiosity. But, I was drawing a blank on how to get there. And, when I saw the dots he was able to connect in his career and free time, it looked pretty damn good. When I shared my desperation with Luke to create a life like his, he encouraged me to take a step back. We were grabbing a coffee one afternoon along the Hudson River in New York and I asked him point blank (quite intensely I might add, likely stemming from my nervousness about life): How do I create a life like yours? How do I get to do what *you* do?

Luke, only about ten years my senior, was kind but forceful in his response: "No, Katina—I think the question you should be asking is what do *you* want to do? What do you want your life to look like? You don't want to just copy mine." He took a pause and looked out to the river before answering. "You studied business in school, right? If you were to create a mission statement for your life, a North Star you can always reach for, what would it sound like?"

I was so caught off guard by his Socratic response I stumbled for a bit to come up with an answer. I finally was able to mumble, "Wow, I've never thought about that before. Um, well, my North Star? I guess I just really want to help people." I pushed myself a little more: "I want to inspire people, young adults really, to live happier and healthier lives. I want them, well all of us, to know it's possible." Luke scratched his beard and nodded his head as my words landed on him. "Hmm," he acknowledged with a far-away look in his eye, "see, that's good. And, that's different than mine, slightly. My North Star is to shift the tides of the world so we all have a fighting chance. No matter where we were born, or what color our skin is. I want all of us to know that we matter—and we can do something about it."

While Luke and I have North Stars with similar roots—to make the world a better place—we each have a different purpose. So, if I just straight up copied Luke's path without reflecting on my own, I wouldn't be fulfilling my passion. I would be trying to shift systems and policies, like he does, instead of working on a human-to-human level. And, to be quite honest I didn't even fully understand that nuance at the time. It took working at a philanthropic venture fund on big societal issues to realize that wasn't how I was meant to make change in the world. But, North Stars don't do the deciding for us, they just help us measure if we're fully aligned.

You might be reading these examples like, okay cool I'm glad you and Luke are so selfless and worldly, but if I were to think about it, my North Star comes nothing close to Changing the World. I care about the beauty of things, or providing stability, or making art. I'm passionate about helping people stay connected or furthering scientific discoveries or even creating a comfortable life for my family. Who knows—that's *exactly* the point. Everyone's North Star is slightly different, and if we just go through life trying to live in someone else's we'll be extremely confused. We'll feel like something just isn't right. So, let's draft yours.

Here's the formula we'll be working from—remember you can just use this as a starting point. Your purpose with this is to create a sentence, a mantra, a mission that helps you measure if you're on *your* path or off. Not *the* Path, but your very unique, very purposeful path. It helps us understand if we're making decisions in alignment with our true purpose and passion or not. Ready?

For context, here's the North Star statement I use to guide all my decisions to this day. It's evolved quite a bit from that pivotal conversation with Luke, but it's relatively the same:

I **create space** for **Millennials** to **mindfully navigate adulthood** so that they can **live happier, healthier, and more meaningful lives.**

But, remember—not everyone is the same. People I've worked with through the On Adulting community have a variety of different passions, purposes, and ways they're creating meaningful lives. And, it doesn't all have to do with work or your career. I personally use my North Star for a variety of different things, whether it's how I volunteer my time or spend it creatively. Now, not everything has to measure up to this Big Life Purpose, but it takes a weight off when you have an ideal to be working toward across different areas of your life.

Let's take some other examples from my coaching clients:

I **use** my humor, empathy, and creativity to **make positive impact** in the world—even for **just one human** being.

I **study** mystical wellness and personal development **for myself and others** to **gain the tools necessary** to **live with more joy and ease** while also leaving room for **excitement and expansion.**

I empower others to **share their story / truth / heart / balance** and **be a positive force in the world.**

It's your turn:

North Star Statement: I **[DO WHAT] [FOR WHO]** to **[HELP THEM WITH WHAT]** so that **[they]** can **[YOUR IDEAL OUTCOME]**.

Your North Star Statement:

I ________ to ________ so that ________.

So, now that you've collected some data from others and done some reflecting about these big life questions yourself, let's start to bring all this dreaming back down to reality. It's all well and good to create these master plans, but what about your everyday life? How does this all factor in to the stuff you do on a regular basis? We're going to start coming down from the clouds a little bit and craft our regular, everyday lives—but we're not leaving Dream World quite yet.

Before we fully land on Earth, I have one more (super fun!) reflection exercise for you to dive into.

What's your Ideal Average Day?

Let go of all senses of reality and dream big with me for a moment:

It's seven o'clock, and the sun is streaming through the open window next to my bed. I slowly roll out of bed, feeling rested for the day ahead. I step out onto my open balcony, and facing the sun I close my eyes to begin my daily meditation practice. After some time, maybe twenty minutes, I set a clear intention for the day and stroll downstairs to the kitchen, where my husband, Dupi, is already having his morning coffee. I sip on some fresh juice and iced coffee, catching up with Dupi about our day ahead. We then both change into workout clothes and do a barefoot exercise in our backyard. Once we're done, we both get ready for the rest of our day.

After a refreshing shower, I take my computer and phone outside—the first time I'm on technology all morning—and begin to dive into writing my next book. I spend about three hours, uninterrupted, in deep work, getting my creative juices flowing. I do this work outside on a comfortable couch, surrounded by nature and light. I know this is my best working style, especially when I'm channeling creativity. I feel so grateful that I have been able to craft a life and a space that allows me to feel my best—and share that experience of being alive with others. After I sense that my brain needs a break, I step inside for a fresh lunch made from our garden. I'm lucky that my husband loves creating meals for us. We have lunch together outside, play with our dog for a bit, and head back to work.

My afternoon is filled with connection—whether that's on phone calls helping people or organizations bend the rules for good, or working on creative projects with Dupi. For another two to three hours, I dive into this type of work style, fulfilling my personal desire to help and connect with others. Around four, I take a walk to grab coffee or a snack—exploring my neighborhood and getting into a new environment. The rest of my evening is spent with Dupi, friends, and relaxing in whatever way feels best. I head to bed, after at least an hour of winding down and reading or painting, fully rested from the day.

Wow—can we just take a minute? Did that Dream World sound like it was straight out of The Kardashians or what?

All joking aside, this excerpt is taken straight from my journal, when I asked myself to dream up my *ideal average day.* I pushed myself to let go of all the rules, all the barriers I put around myself and wondered: if I was just living a regular life, in my best, most fulfilling version of the world, what would it look like? What would my day be filled with? How would I feel at each moment? What types of things would I be doing for work, for nourishment, for connection? How would that be structured? With whom would I be spending my time? These are just a few of the questions I pondered on when I came up with this vision of my Ideal Average Day.

Now, let me be real clear—this is *not* what my day looks like now by any means . . . yet. There are some components, yes, but lunch picked from my garden? If you mean a measly basil plant sitting on my kitchen counter, then sure. A barefoot workout in my yard? I don't even live in a two-bedroom apartment, let alone have *access* to my own green space. But, this type of exercise, one free from reality, is so freakin' fun and insightful it gets me every time. This ability to dream, to create, to craft the everyday life we would dream of if there were no societal rules or barriers feels so good. And, it's another way to collect clues toward what we can begin incorporating into our lives Right Now.

I'm not going to give you any more instruction or chatter for now. I want you to live in this dream world for a little bit longer and reflect on your *ideal average day*. It doesn't need to look remotely at all like mine; in fact, it probably shouldn't. Let all the rules (societal, generational, economic, geographical) go for a moment and reflect on this: If you were to wake up, day after day, like you do right now—what would you want it to look like? If there were no boundaries or rules or bills or forced responsibilities—how would you craft it? Include everything from the tiny details (would you wake up with or without an alarm? What are you eating?) to the big ones (are you by yourself or with humans you care about? How is your day structured? What type of work are you doing—if any?). It literally does not need to fit into any possibility of real life—we'll get to the logistics later.

This exercise might feel uncomfortable or weird, especially when you think about all that's going on in our world at any moment. How could I, lowly me, enter a world where social injustice and rent and climate change not matter? I know those questions bubbled up to the surface for myself as well when I sat down to write this exercise. But, remember: Whether it's an idea or an injustice that keeps tapping you on the shoulder, allow yourself to follow it.

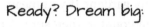

Ready? Dream big:

Take a moment to read through your Dream World. While we might not be able to make this average day happen right now (hey, never say never!), think about this: Are there any aspects of this exercise that surprised you? Stuff you never thought you'd find yourself doing or people you never thought you'd be with? Look back at your Ideal Average Day for clues and jot them down.

The ability for us to conjure up our Ideal Average Day, no matter what our days look like in this moment, is the beauty of being a human. We have the brainpower to dream and create and develop ideas that don't exist yet. And, we know that part of our brain is what makes us unique. So why not use it? Why are we so stuck on following The Path that's been laid out for us?

I wish we could stay in this Dream World forever, but leaving for now and moving into reality—slowly. Before we do, realize this: you just allowed yourself to dream really, really big about what your life *could* be . . . if you let it. You allowed yourself to get creative and let go of some of those "realistic" stories you've been told. You got in touch with your feelings, your purpose, your North Star, and allowed *that* to shine through, over your fears and anxieties. You were no longer paralyzed by "what ifs" and became mesmerized by the possibility of *could* in this Dream World. Let that really, truly soak in.

How could you access this mindset more often? Is it possible for you to tap into this innate creativity of yours in your *real-life average day*? I know it is for sure, I see it all the time, but what might you be resisting? Recognize that everything in your life, in your dreams, is well within your reach. You just need to allow yourself to access it every so often and maybe act on it, too. But, we'll get to that action part now.

— EIGHT —

What Do You *Really* Want?

Do you ever feel like you'll just *never* get off the work-gym-sleep hamster wheel?

If you allow yourself to dream even just a little bit, it's almost as if you're watching a movie of what your life *could* be. It's all fun and games until suddenly, the lights come on and you're dropped back into the kind of world where you sneak popcorn into the theater. It's the feeling when you wake up at dawn on a dreary, winter Wednesday to get ready for work and find yourself scrolling through Instagram before getting out of bed—and wind up in awe and utterly confused at how Sally could afford to do a morning meditation *and* meal-prep her lunch while you can barely find time in your day to get a measly salad. Welcome back to reality, folks.

But, the scariest parts of assessing the hamster wheel is the possibility of getting off. It's what happens when you consider the idea of leaving, when you're teetering at the edge and can see the glistening shores of Mykonos or that new job or whatever your Dream World looks like—and you back out. It's like you're standing at the last step of the high dive as a kid, looking out to the pool dotted with people feet below, and start to back up.

You're so close, but somehow so far away. And, in that split second between thinking and action, fear takes over.

Imagining the idea of actually following our curiosity instead of our very normal, very confusing path—and it *actually* working is sometimes even scarier than staying in the same job for twenty years. We've talked about the concept of fear already, but I know what you're thinking: *What if* you somehow *do* find the courage to step off The Path, and you just end up instead sitting in your fifth-floor walkup studio apartment all alone, with $5 in your bank account and your parents screaming, "I told you so!" over the phone, instead? *What if* you magically end up creating a life that's completely aligned with your passion and purpose, but it all gets taken away when the economy crashes or there's a global pandemic and you need to spend your hard-earned savings on a health emergency? What if, what if, what if patters through your mind any time you live in the Dream World for a second too long.

So, instead of allowing ourselves to imagine the possibilities, we let out a heavy breath and get back on the hamster wheel. We allow the what if's and worst-case scenarios and fear of, well, everything to cloud our dreams. We put our Ideal Day in a tiny little box and only browse through it, wistfully, when we're settled into our very predictable commute. We allow fear and Shoulds and the mundanity of life to dictate our actions. Marianne Williamson, author of *Return to Love: Reflections on the Principles of a Course in Miracles,* once wrote: "Our deepest fear is not that we are inadequate. Our deepest fear is that we are powerful beyond measure. It is our light, not our darkness that most frightens us." Think about that for a moment—our *light*, our plethora of possibilities, is sometimes the scariest option. It's the one that holds us back from actually doing any of the stuff we imagine.

When you reflect on our time together in Dream World last chapter, I'm sure those fears jumped into your brain a few times (or the entire time). Maybe you felt uncomfortable reading through the possibility of seeing your light, but you couldn't place your finger on why. Maybe you (or your Baby Brain) didn't even allow yourself to complete the exercises. Maybe you've seen too many graveyards full of dreams, so without even realizing it you told yourself the same story that's been in your family for generations: "Work is work. *Life* is hard. Reaching for your dreams isn't for everyone."

Growing up, I visited that graveyard of dreams all too often. Even though my family was filled with immigrants and small business owners, two inherently risky ways of being, they were always grasping at the *What Ifs*. On one hand, my parents seemed to create a bubble around my life that truly made me believe *anything* was possible, but in their quiet moments they would mumble about a different type of belief system. I remember hearing these Statements of Settling at the dinner table as a kid over and over again: "Dad *could* have been an engineer, if he just finished college." Or "Mom *could* start her own business, but she just doesn't have any time to do it." When it came to their own lives, my parents seemed to always place so much value on factors outside of their own doing—like a college degree or time or whatever; messages that seemed to be in direct juxtaposition with those "Reach For The Stars" posters plastered on my wall. They, and many other adults I looked up to, often looked at others' success and said with a sigh: "Well, no wonder that I couldn't do what [Sally] is doing—she had [the savings in the bank, no responsibilities holding her back, fill in the blank.]" Those Statements of Settling seeped into my Baby Brain, and over time, made the scary stuff seem much more realistic than my parents would have ever wanted me to believe.

To be clear, I'm not dismissing the very real, very difficult challenges that many of us face in our world where college degrees and time and general privilege equate to sheer livability. We all need to fight to make sure that our access to these opportunities are equal. But, there's also a very real, very important ability to pay attention to the way that our thoughts dictate our actions across the board. Esther Perel, psychotherapist and relationship expert, grew up in post-Holocaust Belgium. Her parents were concentration camp survivors, and she often talks about how her childhood experiences impacted her view of the world. How our perspective and mindset really impact our ability as human beings to live: "I remember, since my entire childhood classroom of children with similar families [to my own], that there were always two groups of families in my community. I decided I would call this . . . well, there was one group that didn't die and one group that came back to life. Those who did not die, you could feel it when you went to their houses. They had plastic all over the couches and the curtains pulled down; it was morbid. You were not dead—but you certainly were not celebrating life. And then, I thought about those who came back to life. How, in the face of adversity, do you continue to imagine yourself rising above it, connected to joy, to love, to pleasure, to beauty, to adventure, to mystery, to all of that?"

And so, even though my parents, and teachers, and the world I grew up in didn't mean to do so, they warped my perception of going for your dreams into one that was practical and pragmatic; it was so rooted in reality that I could barely see the sky. The suburban enclave that was always striving for the next peg of the Great American Dream that I grew up in passed on these messages to us without even recognizing they were doing it: *The world dictates what you're capable of, not you. Life is hard. Work is hard. Reaching for your dreams is impossible.* They craved safety and reliability in their own lives, so any dream we had was often met with that idea-killing question: Is that *realistic*?

I know I'm not alone in this. Neither are my parents. Neither are you. We saw in earlier parts of this book why we as a society are living in a world where Shoulds are prized much more than tapping into our purpose. We learned how our brains are wired to seek safety, to hold onto internalized messages, to be our own domesticators. We've worked through exercises to acknowledge those stories and become aware of them. But, how do we actually act on those reflections—and get out of the prison we created for ourselves?

One of my favorite perspectives on tapping into our authentic selves, regardless of the fear associated, comes from Elle Luna, the creative writer behind the viral *Medium* article and book of the same name, *The Crossroads of Should and Must*. In her book, Elle describes the way we have been conditioned to trap ourselves in the Shoulds of life, or the work-gym-sleep hamster wheel as I like to call it. And in it, she shares the first way we can begin to tap into our Must, or "who we are, what we believe, and what we do when we are alone with our truest, most authentic self."

Before we begin to understand those aspects of our being that makes us feel most alive, consider this perspective from Elle: "If you want to be free—you must understand, first, why you are not free. The word prison comes from the Latin praehendere, meaning to seize, grasp, capture. A prison . . . can be anything your mind creates." Elle then goes on to explain that these prisons we create are from a lifetime of following The Rules, and ultimately, our Baby Brains keeping us safe. But, in order for us to tap into our truest, most authentic self, or our Must, we have to understand what's holding us back. And, oftentimes, "we unconsciously imprison ourselves to avoid our most primal fears. We choose Should because Must is terrifying. And just as you create your prison, you can set yourself free."

Listen, I know that dreaming is scary. Acknowledging that Should Security Guard and peering into the world of Must is even scarier. It's something we're not used to doing; we're so caught up in the prisons of our own creation that we barely allow ourselves to pick our heads up. So maybe, you—like I—have only allowed yourself to dream of this ideal world after what seems like the darkest of moments. And, you might notice that in those moments when you're able to stare fear in the face, everything begins to shift. You're no longer thinking through the list of terrible outcomes but instead, you begin asking yourself that beautiful question: "Well, what's really the worst that could happen?" It could be after a terrible meeting at work, and you somehow find yourself browsing through LinkedIn for jobs in Tokyo instead of sending that follow-up email. Or maybe, it's after your last, fellow single friend tells you that they, too, have entered the dating world that something inside of you tells you that you need to get on those apps once and for all. Leaning into the fear instead of running away from it feels unnatural at first. It probably goes against everything you've ever been taught. But, we're going to learn how to acknowledge our fear, to harness it and shift its energy into the spaces that we want to occupy. We're going to start connecting the dots between where you are Right Now and making the leap into your Dream World—one step at a time.

Fear-setting is the new Goal-setting

If you could describe how fear *feels* or *looks* or *sounds* to you, what would it be like? Would it be a color (for me, dark grey)? A feeling (a mix of butterflies and sheer inability to think or move)? A word (no, no, no, no)? Think back to our exercise in Chapter Five for a moment, and create an image or feeling or word that you associate with fear. What does it do to your body? Your mind? Your overall being?

Fear presents itself differently for every single human on Earth. Even though it might look or feel different for all of us, fear is a real, biological emotion that is universally accepted as a threat of harm to our well-being—whether real or imagined. In the past, psychologists viewed fear as a negative emotion, one that we had to simply *deal* with in our modern world. They hypothesized that while fear may have served a purpose in hunter-gatherer days of our past—like alerting us to predators or helping us cope with natural disasters—it merely gets in the way in a world where we can order food with the click of a button. But, we're coming to learn that if we can channel fear in the right way, if we just simply acknowledge our primal instinct instead of allowing it to make decisions *for* us, fear can become motivating instead of debilitating.

Our ability as humans to analyze and react comes directly from our amygdala, the ancient part of our Baby Brain that is also called "the seat of fear." The amygdala activates our sympathetic nervous system—or the part of our body that chooses to fight or flight. But, the issue that we have with channeling that unconscious response is this: "Change has occurred so rapidly for our species that now we are equipped with brains that are super sensitive to threat but also super capable of planning, thinking, forecasting and looking ahead," says Ahmad Hariri, professor of psychology and neuroscience at Duke University. "So, we essentially drive ourselves nuts worrying about things because we have too much time and don't have many real threats on our survival, so our fear gets expressed in these strange maladaptive ways."

In Chapter Five, we learned how fear, anxiety, and worry have impacted our society, and our generation specifically, when we analyzed the real threats to our safety (or lack thereof) in our modern world. And, during Part 4 we'll dive into some real, quick ways to reduce unwanted fear or worry like let's say, when an ex-boyfriend posts photo after photo with his brand-new partner all over your Instagram feed. But for now, we're going to get to the root of our fears. We're going to dive into a practice that I turn to and recommend to my clients often when they're faced with big life decisions. It's called Fear-Setting (you've heard about it before thanks to our friend Tim F.), which is all about looking our biggest worries right in the face and truly understanding why they're so freakin' scary.

It is, in fact, possible for us to outsmart our primal instincts using tools that help us understand why they're being activated in the first place. So, we're going to go through this exercise as it directly relates to the Dream World you created in the last chapter. If you haven't gone through those exercises yet (damn Baby Brain!) I highly recommend doing so before we practice Fear-setting. Of course, this exercise is meant for you to use many, many times across many different circumstances long after you put this book down, so if you want to dive right in with a different example, go right ahead. But, we'll be using our findings in this chapter to connect the dots between your Life Right Now and Dream World in a little bit.

As a reminder, Fear-Setting is an exercise developed by Tim Ferriss, a podcaster, entrepreneur, author of *The 4-Hour Workweek,* and classic Millennial success story. When Tim found himself paralyzed by a major decision in his life—whether or not to travel while running a high-stress business—he came up with a specific checklist in order to visualize the worst-case scenario and its probability of *actually* happening. He found that all the *What ifs* were spiraling around in his mind, prohibiting him from doing what he actually wanted to do because of made-up (and unlikely) fears. So, instead of allowing them to fester, he decided to do something different. He looked at them head on.

We're going to adapt Tim's checklist and journaling prompts for our own purposes. Nothing against Tim, but his focus is largely on *mitigating* risk, which I find important, but also rooted in fear. We are going to get even deeper than simply just avoiding risk; we're going to look at the root of *why* you're scared, what you can do about it, and if it warrants any further thought—or if you could simply begin letting that shit go.

We're going to work through the following chart to get to the root of our fears using a specific example. You can use anything from your life that feels scary and daunting right now, but the Big Life Question I would recommend reflecting on here is: If you were to start turning your Dream World from Chapter 7 into reality, what might be the most fear-inducing part? Could you put your finger on one (or two or seven) aspects of your dreams that are holding you back?

We're going to move through this adapted version of Fear-setting to assess, honestly, how scary each of these aspects really are. You might notice that as we answer these questions, the fears that run around in your brain and convince you not to do something aren't as scary when we see them up close.

This exercise might be a bit confusing at first, so I've added an example from my own life. When I assessed my Dream World (becoming an author and leaving the corporate world—also known as wearing pants and having a flexible schedule instead of donning an uncomfortable Express suit in front of an Excel spreadsheet), the biggest fear for me circled around money. How would I make it? What would happen if I didn't have any? How could I actually balance the life that I wanted with the sacrifices I'd seemingly have to make?

Money is a topic that holds a lot of baggage for us humans—and we'll dive into that much deeper during the next chapter—but for now let's work through our fears on all fronts. Take some time to consider: *What's the worst that could happen?*

What is the Worst Possible Outcome [WPO]? (There can be many!)	**How would you feel if this WPO actually happened?**	**What is the realistic likelihood of this WPO actually occurring?**
I don't have any money	Really sad and scared	Pretty unlikely; I'm sure I could figure out a way to make money somehow
Other examples: I fail and am out of a job / I can never go back to getting a regular job again		
Other examples: My parents are upset with me		
Any other examples you could come up with—go!		

If the WPO *did* happen, what would be your first reaction?	**How might you solve this WPO if it did happen?**	**Taking a step back, how scary is this possibility (using our 1 to 10 scale)?**
I would be scared at first, but then I would figure it out	I would make a spending and savings plan so I become more aware of what's going out / in I would find a way to bring in some extra income, even if it means sacrificing some time / doing something I don't want to	4/10: It's definitely still scary, but something I could manage

As you can see, scary stuff isn't *that* scary when you hold a light to it. And heck, sometimes it is. Sometimes, it's real and scary and possible. But, it stings a little less when we can look at it in the eye. It's almost like the old days when you'd run into your room after watching *Aaahh!!! Real Monsters* in the complete dark (no cell phones to lead the way back then), worried that Ickis or Krumm is chasing you. But then, you see your glow-in-the-dark stars above your bed—a tiny, sparkling glow that can make you feel a little less alone.

Now, this Fear-setting practice isn't the be-all end-all to our scary issues. But, it's a starting point that will help illuminate some of the secrets and *What Ifs* that lurk in the dark. It helps us get to the root of our well-meaning primal response to a potentially very scary situation—the deepest part of us whose sole intention is to keep us safe. Because sometimes, our Baby Brains get the wires crossed; our brain's Seat of Fear tries to protect us from something that isn't actually all that scary. Being able to become conscious and aware of everything as it is, is truly liberating, not the stories our brains create based on the beliefs we've been told our entire lives.

So, what do you *really* want? Where did fear possibly cloud your vision? If you're up for it, revisit your Dream World reflections with this new information. As you do, recognize that fear and desire, worry and motivation can (and often do) co-exist together. As Dr. Tsabary told us in Chapter Three, our feelings are fleeting waves that wash over us at random. They do not define us. And usually, seeing those feelings, like fear, up close dissipates their hold on us.

If and when you go back to your Dream World armed with this new set of knowledge about yourself, this new layer of beliefs peeled back, try to see what was written in between the lines. Maybe during your *Ideal Average Day* you sold yourself short a bit.

Maybe you only allowed yourself to think of ideas that were well within your reach. Maybe you can push yourself to dream a little bit more, with fear right by your side.

We're (still) in the Messy Middle

So, now what? We've started feeling our feelings, telling the truth, dreaming big, and acknowledging our fears—what do we do next? A lot of my clients call all this reflecting The Messy Middle. Because, it is messy! It's weird and confusing to begin to unpack our long-held beliefs. It's uncomfortable to become aware of the stuff we've been holding onto for a while. And, I want to make sure to acknowledge how weird and confusing and uncomfortable that may be.

So, if you are feeling confused right now, you're on the right path. You might find yourself resisting going any further. You might want to slam this book shut as you hear your subway stop blaring out and walk to work in a blur. You may go to sleep after working through some exercises and feel unsettled. I know, I've been there. And honestly if that feeling resonates with you, then that's a good sign: you're diving into the amazing, rewarding ability to finally see your true, authentic self.

Be sure to acknowledge it. Feel those feelings. Find a way to move through it; tap into some of those practices you learned about in earlier chapters—or ones that you've always turned to during times of change. It could be journaling or painting or moving your body. Whatever it is, think of this as your reminder to connect with You, and understand what stuff is coming up.

'Cause we're about to dive into the most *fun* topic in adulthood we've yet to talk about: Money and Responsibilities.

NINE

Mo' Money, Mo' Problems

How often have you talked yourself out of looking at your bank account, because you're scared of what you might see?

There was a period of time when I was literally scared shitless to check my bank statement, so much so that I'd pour myself a glass of wine before doing it. It felt like I was preparing for an intimidating meeting at work, and sometimes, it rose to the level of anxiety I experienced when I told my parents that I was seriously dating a Punjabi guy instead of a nice, Greek boy from Brooklyn, like they always wished. This monthly occurrence brought me so much stress that I often would find any excuse I could *not* to check—as if pretending that my credit card didn't exist would somehow make it disappear.

Reflecting on that time now, there was no logical reason to be that worried. Upon graduating from college, I was fortunate enough to have a stable job, and a well-paying one at that. Unlike most of my peers, the first time I ever got a credit card was a few months after entering the Real World—with the intention of "increasing my credit score," not buying $500 worth of clothes at Forever 21. Up until then, my parents only encouraged me to use a debit card or the cash I received from my tutoring jobs so that I never overextended myself financially. I was oddly cautious in that way. If I didn't physically have the money, I didn't understand why I would spend it. I grew up in a very money-aware household; we were constantly checking price-tags whether we were at the supermarket or Marshalls. So, I was extremely particular about what went on my credit card (reoccurring payments like Netflix, and small, manageable charges like my daily coffee runs) versus debit (big purchases like travel or a splurge-worthy dinner). But still, even though I was keeping a mental checklist of how many $5 cold brews I could buy as a break from work before I reached my self-imposed limit, checking my bank account each month brought me immense stress. When I finally mustered the courage to stare those numbers in the face, it took all my self-restraint *not* to close the tab if the log-in process took more than five seconds.

What I didn't realize at the time was that I was experiencing financial anxiety—real, crippling anxiety around managing money and all the adult stuff I was suddenly thrust into doing. I was worried that I wouldn't be able to pay my loans on time, or invest enough into my 401K. What if I missed a rent payment or my Excel monthly budget was suddenly in the red? For so long, I had been telling myself the same story: "I don't have money to do [fill in the blank]. My savings account has like $3 in it (literally). No, I *definitely* can't take that trip or go to that dinner. Should I walk instead of take the subway? I think I have to save that ride to go Uptown." The list of excuses, worries, and fears could go on for pages and pages—but I'll spare you (or maybe, you could fill in the details with your own).

In my case, I first became financially independent from my parents when I became a college student in New York City, one who was on partial scholarship and was accruing loans just to *be* there—so, I crafted a story that I never had enough. I was always in comparison mode (Oh, *she* has a trust fund, so that's why she could go shopping in SoHo) and full of lack. So, when I finally had thousands of dollars trickling into my very starved bank account each month, I was worried that I would fuck it up.

My own concerns around finances, and all the responsibilities that come along with entering this club we never asked to join aren't unique. Because while, yes, it's nice to live in a Dream World where we all have houses with backyards and pools and chefs who make us green juice from our garden every morning, last time I checked we're Millennials here on Earth. And, Earth is filled with bank accounts and loan payments and laundry that builds up over time instead. And, we have real reasons to be worried. Millennials are the first generation to experience a lower standard of living than their parents. We are collectively in almost $500 *billion* of student loan debt—with the average person paying down $33,000 of loans. We have financial obligations that require us to be at our very boring, very stable jobs—not some Instagram influencer living in Bali.

I know what you're thinking: this is the boring chapter filled with all the shit that you'd rather do the *New York Times* crossword puzzle seven times over than think about. Taxes, apartments, and Excel budgeting documents are *no fun*. You know, all the "adulting" stuff that falls onto our lap once we arrive into The Club. And hey, I'm not going to lie—we are in fact going to dive into all the boring stuff we're required to do once we get here for the next little while. But, like everything else in this book, I'm not going to tell you exactly *how* to pay your bills on time or finish off your loans before you're twenty-five; we're going to work through the ways to create change for the rest of your life.

I spent a long time trying to "hack" my way into saving money and becoming financially abundant. I read all the blogs I could on achieving financial stability and went to every financial support workshop that was offered at school or work, but it wasn't until I addressed this deep-seeded mentality of lack that I actually solved my issues. It literally didn't matter how much money I had in the bank, whether I was scrambling for my last twenty-five cents to grab a banana for dinner or investing thousands of dollars into the stock market. Once I found my true worthiness when it came to money, and started to *trust myself*, I was able to pay off thousands of dollars in loans *and* funnel tens of thousands of dollars into savings—all before the age of twenty-five. And, you already know my parents were definitely not giving me any help there.

Even though I can give you very specific instructions on the best bank when it comes to saving money or how to accrue credit card points, I won't. For one, I'm sure this information will become outdated a month or two after this book is published. And most importantly, it doesn't solve our core issues in the first place. So, I'm going to take you through the process of shifting how you approach the boring stuff to make it, dare I say, *fun* instead.

Is Biggie Right?

I might have to disagree with Biggie on this one. Even though, yes, it's true that money doesn't solve our problems (and may seem to create more), the stuff we believe about money stems from our damn Baby Brain (seriously, again!). That means more money might illuminate our issues, but they've been there for a *long* time, my friend.

Think about it for a moment: when I say the word *money* what do you think? Jot down any ideas you associate with the green stuff—without judgment. Allow your thoughts to flow, simply:

For a long time, I thought about money like this: *It was evil, but necessary. If I had more of it (the most of it) I would be happy. I would be free. I could do whatever the hell I wanted. Getting money took hard work and a long time to get it. I needed it in order to buy the stuff I wanted—that would ultimately make me cool, interesting, likable. Money (and all the stuff that came with it) equaled success. In order to get it, I'd have to do stuff that I didn't like doing at all—because art or creativity or making a positive impact on the world didn't have any money in it. That could come later. But now? I didn't have any of it, and I needed it so I'd have to sacrifice. And, I was always struggling to keep it. Money scared the shit out of me and I never, ever, ever felt like I had enough.*

Do any of these ideas ring a bell for you? If you're nodding your head like *"hell yes woman you **get** me!"* you're not alone. Money is one of the weirdest, most confusing aspects of being a human today. I love the way Jen Sincero describes it in her book, *You Are A Badass At Making Money*: "When it comes to having sex or making money, you're supposed to know what you're doing and be all great at it, and you're never supposed to talk about it because it's inappropriate, dirty, not so classy. Both money and sex can provide unthinkable pleasures, birth new life, and inspire violence and divorce. We're ashamed if we don't have it, we're even more ashamed to admit that we want it."

One of the biggest shifts that I experienced in adulthood was changing my relationship with money. Once I confronted those fears and anxieties—that by the way, were lurking in the corners no matter how much of it I had—I entered a state of flow across so many areas of my life. I never imagined I'd get to a place of freedom and confidence (and paying off my student loans) while still in my mid-twenties, but when I got real about the money stories I was telling myself, something within me shifted. My worth began to align with the way I saw money—as an infinite resource rather than it being this elusive thing I was always chasing, but could somehow never find. So, we're going to work through some of those stories you've been telling yourself, no matter how much dough is in your bank account right now. Because, money isn't just about success or traveling or retiring at thirty. It gets to the core of all the work we've been doing together so far—as our friend Jen says, "It's about creating the wealth that affords you the life you'd love to live instead of settling for what you think you can get."

Money is just a green piece of paper (or a picture on your phone)

As you've seen, we make up a lot of shit in our minds about stuff that we're scared of. Stuff that we're confused about. Stuff that we don't fully understand. And, if you think about it from the most objective point of view: money is literally a piece of paper. It's a piece of paper with the most baggage I've ever seen, but that's what it is at its core. Us humans are the ones who create all these stories around it. Our Baby Brains are constantly feeding us these warped visions of money based on what we saw growing up or experiences we've had. So, since this entire part of our time together is about working through the stuff that makes adulthood weird instead of fun, we're going to look every potential story about money in the eye and figure out why we might think that way. We're continuing to peel back the layers, one belief system at a time.

Every single one of these stories might not directly relate to your own lived experience. And, that's cool. But, how can it further challenge the perception you have around money? How can you work on viewing money as what it simply is: an infinite resource that's not inherently bad or good, just simply a tool to help us do the stuff we want to in life; a resource that helps us be our truest, most authentic selves on this windy road of growing up?

Let's dive in to assessing all the baggage our Baby Brains believe about money. I'll fill in an example about how I'd work through this exercise, and then you're off to the races. I've laid out some of the most common stories, beliefs, and worries around money that I've heard from the On Adulting community. So, we'll think about those first—really challenge yourself to assess if this is a story that you hold onto in any depths of your Baby Brain or not. And then, you'll have space to hash through your own:

Katina's example: I'm running out of money and I never have enough

What that means to me:

I feel like no matter what I do, money will never be there. I always have to skimp and save no matter what number I see in my bank account. I never allow myself to enjoy little pleasures, like coffee or a workout class with a friend, out of fear that one day something will happen where I'll need to use my savings and I'll regret it.

Why you might believe it:

Growing up, it always felt like money was never enough. I was always looking at price tags and was really aware about spending habits. I was taught that I should never run into a situation where I don't have enough money, so I was scared of spending "frivolously"—which meant not spending money at all.

How you can practice shifting this mindset:

Maybe I can buy myself something small, just to get comfortable with it, like a weekly coffee at my favorite coffee shop? Maybe I can even tip on top of that, too, because I know that giving money to others only shows me that I believe in its infinite ability to show up in my life, and help others along the way.

Story Number One: I'm running out of money and I never have enough

What that means to me:

Why you might believe it:

How you can practice shifting this mindset:

Story Number Two: I have to sell my soul in order to get it

What that means to me:

Why you might believe it:

How you can practice shifting this mindset:

Story Number Three: I will never be able to use it for what I want

What that means to me:

Why you might believe it:

How you can practice shifting this mindset:

Story Number Four: It's scary to think about so I just avoid it completely

What that means to me:

Why you might believe it:

How you can practice shifting this mindset:

Story Number Five: Once I have a lot of it, I'll feel happy and free

What that means to me:

Why you might believe it:

How you can practice shifting this mindset:

Another $$ story you have:

What that means to me:

Why you might believe it:

How you can practice shifting this mindset:

Money is simply a reflection of our values

Now, shifting our beliefs about money is only part of the battle. Some of you might be like, "Well, this is great, but I have rent payments to make and thousands of dollars in loans and I want to quit my soul-sucking job. How does thinking about my stories around money help me right now?" While yes, these mindset shifts are a *long-term* practice—one that doesn't make your loans disappear tomorrow—they are the foundation of how we begin to practice living a life *full* of wealth. Shifting our belief system is how we make all that boring stuff fun. And, not only fun, but really have the power to change our lives.

At the end of the day, money, or laundry, or anything that you really, really don't want to think about is simply an exchange of *value*. It's a practice in placing our energy on stuff or experiences or types of work that we think are important. And, a lot of times as we enter adulthood, for good reason, we don't necessarily think about the value of money from a grounded perspective. We humdrum along, going out to a fancy dinner with mediocre co-workers or getting a new pair of shoes because we feel like ones from last season are outdated.

Just consider for a moment the last purchase you made. Hold it in your mind and think about the following: Before you bought it, did you think about *why* you needed or wanted it, or was it something you mindlessly brought to the checkout counter—physically or digitally if you catch my drift? That reason doesn't need to be anything other than *this makes me feel good right now,* but you'd be surprised at how many times we basically throw our money away without even realizing it.

Becoming conscious and mindful about how we view money feels very different than how most of us have been raised, and it's intimidating to practice at first. Because, while traditional budgeting and financial advice may tell us *not* to treat ourselves with a daily cup of coffee in order to save for that house or pay off our loans, I beg to differ. Money is a constant representation of how we choose to see our own self-worth. It's always evolving, and trust me, it will continue to ebb and flow throughout our lives.

My favorite way to think about money as a mindful resource is similar to our food pyramid. I created it when I was trying to

Our gifts
These are choices that can help others in our community
Our Treats
Stuff that we find enjoyable, and might happen less often
Our Well-Being
This is the stuff that makes us feel good on a regular basis.
Our Needs
This is the stuff we need to survive in this world.

figure out how to value the way that I allocated this resource that felt so new, and simultaneously so confusing to me. The Wealth Nourishment Pyramid, as I like to call it, has one purpose: to provide a visual representation to our needs, wants, and desires—and the value that we associate with each of them.

The most interesting part about our Wealth Nourishment Pyramid is that it's completely fluid and everchanging. I like to think about the Wealth Nourishment Pyramid in four different components. The first is "Our Needs." This is simply the stuff we need to survive in this world. It's financial obligations that will exist no matter if we're CEO of a major company or living out with Sally as a yoga teacher in Bali. Some examples of these obligations include: healthcare, taxes, transportation, housing, and any loans that we might have. The middle layer is "Our Well-being." This is the stuff that makes us feel good on a regular, everyday basis. We interact with these purchases frequently, and this category is the most fluid. It's usually where we tend to make the most trade-offs (if we're aware of them). We'll go into an example of this in a moment, but think of the following buckets as a starting point: our workouts, food and drink spending, and how we connect with our friends or family—whether that's at happy hour or over Zoom. Our top-most category is called "Our Treats," and this group of spending includes anything we consciously view as a special occurrence that truly brings us joy or utility. Some examples of spending in this category might be technological upgrades, shopping (for fun), or travel. Lastly, my favorite category is something that's dispersed throughout our Wealth Nourishment Pyramid: "Our Gifts." A lot of times, we forget how important it is to spread our wealth—even if we only have twenty-five cents to buy a banana. This category is a reminder for all of us that money is an infinite resource, and we don't need to hoard everything we have "just in case" something happens. We can share it in any way that feels true to our lives at the moment—whether helping with our parent's car payments, tipping our local barista or donating to an organization that is creating impact in our community.

The key point through all of this? There are no hard lines to draw, and we are constantly evaluating our conscious decision-making. For example, think about this: We all understand there are things we need to spend money on in order to sustain our life, like housing, healthcare, and food, but these aspects of our nourishment wealth pyramid can vary based on our values at any given time. We might choose to live in a really nice apartment, because we work from home and spend our entire day there. Or maybe having a grounding space is vital to your overall happiness. Or maybe, we don't care about our living situation at all because we work all the time, so we choose to save by living with four roommates. Based on this conscious decision, there may be other tradeoffs we need to make. If we choose to splurge on our monthly rent, we may make dinner every night instead of going out. Or maybe we choose to create a makeshift gym in said apartment, instead of adding another monthly membership to our bills. Or maybe we eat out on the weekends, because it makes us really happy but decide to stock up our fridge from the supermarket all week. The tradeoffs exist everywhere, as long as we're paying attention and acting from a place of values instead of comparison.

For me, buying an afternoon cup of coffee at my local coffee shop brings me so much joy I honestly can't put a price on it. Some of you might gawk at spending $4.50 on essentially black water filled with ice, but for me it represents so much more than just simply drinking coffee. Getting coffee during the work day allows me to take scheduled "me" time, even if it's only ten minutes. It reminds me to step away from my desk, to get in touch with my thoughts, to build relationships with people outside of work or home (my baristas know more about me than some of my friends), and to demonstrate to myself that, yes, I am worth this *treat*.

We all have different versions of our treats. We all have different things that bring us joy, that signal to us money is more than just a result of our never-ending run on the work-gym-sleep hamster wheel. But, the key aspect of this mindset is that treats are special; we're not constantly treating ourselves to splurge-worthy vacations on European islands while *also* dwindling our savings accounts on fancy lunches each day. And, remember: treats don't need to be extravagant. They don't even need to cost anything, truly, like shifting your commute spending to a one-time bike purchase instead of daily train rides so you can get some exercise in, too. Or you could think of these shifts as "buying" yourself time—like investing in a nicer vacuum (how adult of you) so that you can save energy on cleaning, instead, gifting yourself a little extra sleep on the weekends.

Now it's your turn to make your own Wealth Nourishment Pyramid. As you go through it, you might ask yourself a few questions: What aspects of your life are you prioritizing right now? What tradeoffs might you make in the moment—and how might that change over time? Are there treats that you're able to sprinkle in that allow you to raise your self-worth, joy, and overall happiness? How can you think about releasing your tight grip on this continuous resource that's always available to you and share it with others in need?

You might simply start by recreating how you typically spend right now. That might be enough of an exercise (trust me, I know how stressful it is to even think about money, let alone plan for the future). But, if you're ready to begin thinking more consciously about your relationship with wealth, you may try this exercise twice: once with a view of your habits at the moment, and another with potential trade-offs and conscious decisions you can begin to make.

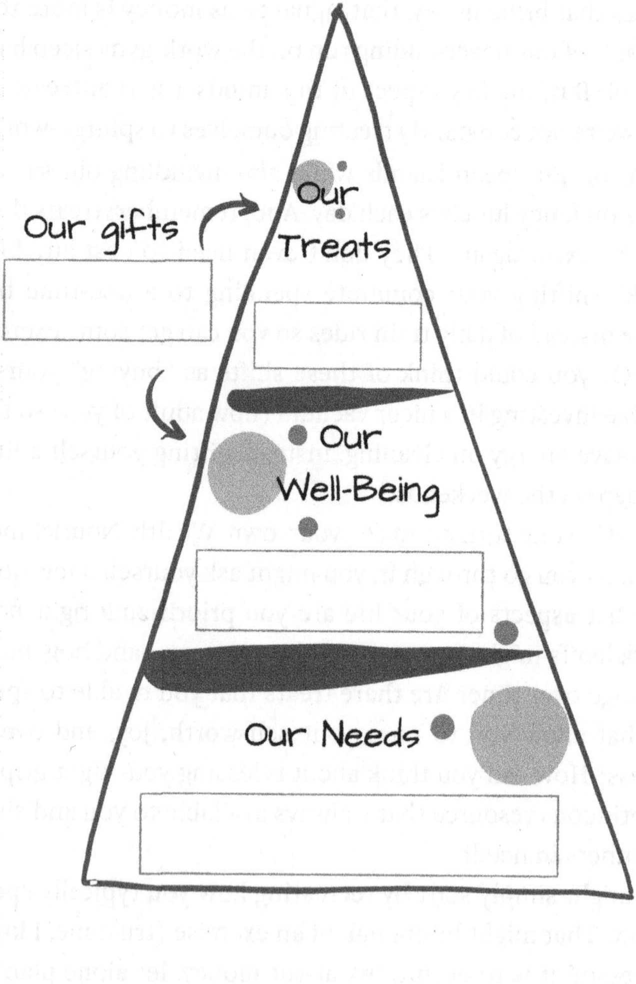

Now that we've had some time to assess your beliefs around the boring, stressful parts of Adulting and map out your values in the right now, you can take a deep breath. We're slowly and clearly making our way out of the tunnel. We're crafting a realistic-but-idealistic life for ourselves that's rooted in both honesty and imagination, even when it comes to one of the most confusing parts of growing up, our finances.

So, we're going to keep moving along and tackle another big question mark that circles around Adulthood: the everchanging flow of relationships. Here's a preview: not all of the difficult ones need to end by ghosting the human on the other side.

— TEN —

Changing You Means Changing Relationships, Too

Have you ever questioned why certain people are still in your life?

That might sound harsh, but it's one of those icky, uncomfortable thoughts that slips into the front of your mind as quickly as you try to make it disappear. Maybe it's when your childhood best friend seems to only feign excitement when you announce your promotion at work, and somehow you feel like a burden and a self-absorbed braggadocio all at once. Or maybe it's when your long-term boyfriend suggests going to dinner (again) at the local restaurant in your town, even though you'd rather *treat yourself* to a workout class or weekend trip, but you can't seem to work up the courage to say it. Or possibly—this one's the worst—it's when you hear your mom or dad rambling on and on over the phone about the same small-town drama that consumed you for so long, but now you see it for what it is: a waste of time and energy.

One of the less satisfying and simultaneously most confusing aspects of adulthood is recognizing the everchanging essence of human relationships. As we become awake to our own authenticity, our own truths, we suddenly see the world in an entirely new light. And, that slowly begins to ripple out to the way we spend our time, the people we interact with, and the communities we build. Friends whom you imagined would be your forever people begin to disappear into the background. Even your parents or siblings could be cast in a new, slightly murky perspective. When we begin to wake up, when we start to imagine what our lives *could* look like instead of resigning ourselves to the path that's laid out before us, we shed many parts of our past selves. And one of the most heartbreaking, difficult, and simultaneously refreshing aspects of that process is cultivating relationships that reflect who we are and who we want to be, not who we once were.

The first time this ever happened to me, I felt like my world was ending. Growing up in my small suburban town, I had a very strong, very cliquish (we'll use that word nicely) group of girlfriends. We called ourselves the Nine Betches. Yes, seriously—we even had a private Facebook *and* texting group of the same name. We did *everything* together—we picked out our prom dresses together, went on vacations together, gossiped about weird boys at school together, had our first sips of our parents' vodka together (and then, got caught together). We knew each other's deepest secrets and desires. They saw me at my best (which my seventeen-year-old self might argue that was at a high school basement party, and *not* on stage accepting honor roll awards 'cause that was lame) and my worst, which we can all agree was that one time I hit my brother with an iHome console for reasons I will not name here (no freakin' joke, anyone with younger brothers will catch my drift). Back then, I could never imagine a time when we wouldn't be best friends. I couldn't see outside of our insulated world where a disproportionate amount of people married their high school sweetheart and families lived in the same exact house their parents grew up in.

When I got to college—only a few miles from this very town, but truly a world away—I didn't have any expectations that my life or relationships would change. Quite honestly and now embarrassingly, I silently judged those who would show up to a freshman orientation session and willingly admit that they were "floaters" in high school, their desperation for the very types of relationships I already had as a teen was so open and raw. And, instead of seeing this experience as a new opportunity to connect with those who challenged my world view, I dismissed them without even giving them a chance. I ran home to my comfort zone—my friends and boyfriend—who reinforced the weirdness and newness I was experiencing. My childhood friends fed me the same stories that I had heard my entire life, and that felt much better than actually going through the effort to connect with new people.

It didn't take long for me to get a nudge, a feeling deep in my gut that I was changing. Only a few weeks into my first semester of college I remember going home for Thanksgiving and feeling so relieved to be surrounded by that sense of comfort once again. It was *almost* as if nothing had changed: The Nine Betches got ready together and headed to another friend's basement for a Natty Lite-infused evening of "catching up" with the rest of our high school crew. But, on our drive over to the party one of the girls yelled over Z-100 blasting in the background (a little tipsy from one too many Mike's Hard Lemonades): "Guys—I love you all *so much*. I can't wait until we graduate from college and get married and buy houses on the same block. Which block should we live on?!"

What ensued was the first crack in a crumbling mountain of change for me; as the rest of The Betches contemplated which block had the best access to sun *and* the highway to the beach, I found myself staring off into the distance. Only a few weeks of living alone in New York City, taking in all the sights and sounds and people that were so different than those quiet, tree-lined blocks in our town, made me question if that's truly what I wanted. In that twilight zone-esque moment, a bit tipsy from our parents' alcohol with my supposed best friends in the entire world, I saw the future that they were describing flash in front of my eyes, and every cell within me rejected it. There was a tremor beginning to shake within me, a vision that was building from the cracks, and heck, it didn't look the same as everyone else's in that car. But, in that car I couldn't see that future. I could only process feeling sad and alone. I felt like something was wrong with *me*. It was the beginning of the end.

It only took one more year for my first friend (and subsequent boyfriend) break-up to come to fruition. After that seemingly innocent evening, I began to notice many more cracks—ideas or thoughts or experiences that didn't necessarily align with who I was becoming. As I was being exposed to all these different world views it seemed like The Nine Betches were staying exactly the same. Which, in hindsight, is totally okay. But, at the time my nineteen-year-old-self couldn't have been more resentful—at them and at myself. Because, I wanted so badly to be interested in the same things that they were, that I once was. But, annoying little comments I would brush off ("Wow Katina, you're reading your Kindle at the beach instead of talking to us *again*") started to get under my skin. So, I began hanging out with them less and less. I stopped answering in the group chat. I started, almost subconsciously, to miss group birthday dinners and those random hangouts that I used to crave. As my world view began to shift, I didn't know how to handle the confusing feelings I was having. Some might say "we grew apart" but as I reflect on it now, instead of sharing the changes I was experiencing, I ghosted my very best friends out of pain, sadness, and self-preservation.

My growth from The Nine Betches wasn't the only time in my life that I've experienced a shift in relationships. It's happened many more times than I would have expected, though not all of them felt like such a heavy weight was crashing around me. Each time it happens, whether it's because of a move to a new city, or uncovering a difference in values I didn't see before, I hope that it will be the last time—though I know that's not the case. But, the more that I've practiced standing in my worth, becoming aware of my deepest values, and most importantly, recognizing the aspects of myself that I personally need to work on, I've come to view relationships—no matter how long they're in our lives—as mirrors for our own. Each human being that we build a connection with can be a teacher for us; we just need the tools in our metaphorical toolbox to view it that way.

It's in our DNA

Before we convince ourselves that we're not *here* to make friends anyway (circa Real World 2001), let's be clear about one thing: connecting with other humans is a vital aspect of our health and longevity. Think about how good it feels when you're able to unwind from a long day by laughing with your roommate on your tiny IKEA couch, or having a deep conversation with a random person at a party. Connecting with other human beings doesn't just feel good—it's actually a major aspect of our survival as a species. Our brains are literally hardwired for it. From the moment babies take their first breath, they cry and reach for their mothers. As we grow, our craving for connection shifts from mere survival to deeper, nuanced relationships—but the need is always there. Brené Brown, a world-renowned researcher, speaker on social connections, and guest star in the rom-com *Wine Country*, explains how integrated human connection is to our DNA: "A deep sense of love and belonging is an irresistible need of all people. We are biologically, cognitively, physically and spiritually wired to love, to be loved, and to belong. When those needs are not met, we don't function as we're meant to."

Unfortunately, we've been seeing that disfunction take precedence a lot lately. Our modern society, especially in the West, has come so far from the idea of "it takes a village" and instead replaced it with the belief that we alone are responsible for our success and survival. Long-standing institutions, from media to education systems, have even been structured to enforce these ideas especially in the United States. This comparison written in the *New York Times* over two decades ago draws drastic differences in belief systems between the United States and Japan and still holds true today: "While Americans say the squeaky wheel gets the grease, in Japan the maxim is 'the nail that sticks out gets pounded down.' And while American children who don't finish their food are given stern warnings not to waste it, Japanese children are told, 'Think about how bad the farmer who raised this food for you will feel if you don't eat it.'" For most of us reading this book, I bet we've been raised with the idea that we don't *need* anyone else. I mean, just look at some of the common themes from popular reality shows today—you may laugh, but one could argue they are a true mirror of our society. We often hear the same types of complaints and reassurances: "I'm not here to make friends" is such a common phrase, it has its own YouTube video compilation that's over ten minutes long.

But, this isn't necessarily our fault. Our world today is set up to make us addicted to fake connections. Researchers recently conducted a study on what "connecting" on social media does to our brain and found that when we receive likes on Instagram or a message on Snapchat, the dopamine in our brain spikes. We become addicted to the attention, rather than the connection. And, due to these shifts in how we connect with others, we've lost our ability to create relationships in real life. We already know that loneliness is a rising epidemic, but it has an actual impact on our health and well-being. We stand on the subway with our face in our phones. We wait for a friend to show up at a bar completely avoiding eye contact with other physical humans, only to "connect" with other people superficially, through a screen. We ghost budding relationships because they don't fit our version of "perfect." Even though on the surface, it might *feel* like we're building relationships, over 70 percent of adults today say they have only *one* close friend. One. And, more than half of Americans say that they're lonely *most* of the time. We can't just hit up that random person we were messaging on Bumble for help moving out of our apartment or if we need a ride to the doctor. Real, deep social connections allow our society to thrive. And, researchers have been finding that the increase of "loose" social connections leads to major health risks—ranging from heart disease to anxiety disorders. Some say that loneliness is akin to smoking 15 cigarette packs per day.

It's not all bad news though. We don't even have to go *that* far out of our way to connect with other human beings, either: a simple hello to your coffee barista, or even making eye contact with a stranger on the subway is proven to have long-lasting benefits. Human connection is powerful in any form, even the tiny moments you might typically skip over. Emma Seppla of the Stanford Center for Compassion and Altruism has found through her research that "people who feel more connected to others have lower levels of anxiety and depression. Moreover, studies show they also have higher self-esteem, greater empathy for others, are more trusting and cooperative, and, as a consequence, others are more open and trusting to them." So, even if we look at it from the most individualistic lens, building real, strong relationships are vital.

This is the first time you'll hear me say this, but our expectations need to be much lower

Sometimes, our inherent craving for deeper connection than just the number of followers on our Instagram can blind us to the reality of what that relationship brings to our lives. Our good friend and relationship therapist, Esther Perel, has often led discussions on podcasts and the TED stage alike, about this modern conundrum. Let's take her explanation of marriage, for example: "Marriage was an economic institution in which you were given a partnership for life in terms of children and social status and succession and companionship. Now we want our partner to fill all of those things, but in addition, I want you to be my best friend and trusted confidant and my passionate lover to boot. And . . . we live twice as long."

Esther's observation about our expectations for our romantic relationships extends to many other forms of human connection we seek out—not just our long-term life partners. On one hand, we're extremely antisocial—enforcing our ability and need to be independent. But, on the other hand we seek our partners and friends and family members to fill each and every one of our needs. We hold them in the highest standards and expect that one friend, that one connection to represent what an entire village once would. And so, you can imagine where the problems begin to ensue.

We're going to begin to analyze and unwind some of those expectations together. Because, the only way that we can start building authentic connections that are vital to our very existence is if we understand what we have right now. Think about it—when was the last time you consciously assessed the relationships in your life? Have you ever actively thought that you have *choice* over the people that you spend time with?

In the following exercise, we're going to plot four different relationship segments: personal, familial, romantic, and friendships. Each of these quadrants are super important to our existence—they make up our metaphorical village. And, we're going to ask ourselves two different questions about each of these sections. First, is this "group" of people aligned with my personal values—regardless if I feel like I have choice in my relationship with them or not? And second, am I focusing too much or too little on this area? Now, the tricky part of all this is that human relationships are dynamic. We may find that we're focusing a *ton* on our familial section right now, because we have an aging parent or sibling in need. Or maybe, we're deeply focused on our personal section—you might have a big personal move coming up or career growth you care about. While it's really important for us to find balance in our relationships, we can also recognize that we have seasons of life that shift and change as we do, too.

Before we dive in, let's think a bit about the importance of determining relationship values. Each group in our metaphorical village is meant to fulfill different needs in our life. For example, according to recent scientific findings, friendships are collectively defined as having three main qualities: they are long-lasting, positive, and cooperative. While on the other hand, romantic relationships bring a different lens of characteristics, such as trust, vulnerability, and affection, in order for them to thrive. But, regardless of where this person sits in our village, there are a few commonalities that should be present in all of our relationships. I like the way that clinical psychologist and author, Carla Marie Manly, PhD., explains that there are six key factors in any healthy relationship: need, desire, ability, willingness, availability, and commitment. These are the foundational building blocks for any relationship, though they may vary depending on where they sit in our village.

My definition is a bit simpler. To me, relationships should make us feel three things no matter what: safe, free, and respected. You may come up with your own key values. But most importantly if certain connections don't meet those criteria right away or at all times, that doesn't mean I ghost them immediately like I did when I was twenty. I view it as an opportunity to communicate my values and stand in my worth by drawing boundaries. We'll talk through boundary-setting and communication when it comes to relationships in a bit, but let's dive in and begin to assess each area of our relationships first. From there, we can decide how to make changes as needed.

In the matrix below, you'll want to assess each area of your relationships based on two main components: personal or collective values and time spent. You may want to get creative here and make this your own—possibly by color-coding different flavors of relationships or areas you want to work on. I'll leave this up to you to define. This tool is a starting point for many different aspects of reflection and subsequent changes you might make based on the results you see here.

Your Metaphorical Village

The three most important values when it comes to my relationships:

1.
2.
3.

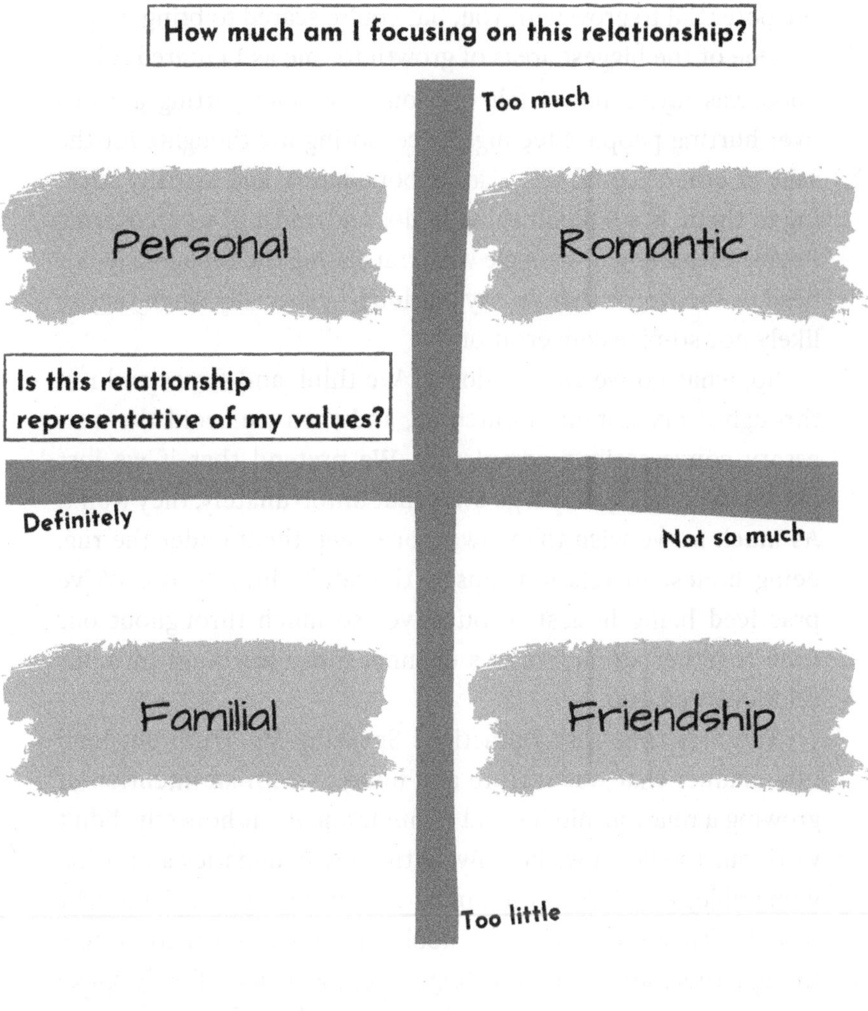
How much am I focusing on this relationship?
Too much
Personal
Romantic
Is this relationship representative of my values?
Definitely
Not so much
Familial
Friendship
Too little

Don't hide your truth

Okay, so now what? Maybe there's one section of your matrix that has *glaring* issues, but you don't know how to handle it. Or maybe you can now see that there's a part of your village that has the potential to grow with you, but you're scared to bring it up.

One of the biggest areas of growth for me as I entered Adulthood was *saying* how I felt out loud—without getting anxious over hurting people's feelings or censoring my thoughts for the sake of others' comfort. Creating boundaries, and actually sticking to them, is a difficult thing to do. And, most of us recovering People Pleasers will struggle with translating the thoughts in our head to the words that we say out loud—especially when they're likely not-so-nice conversations.

So, what do we end up doing? We think and stress and run through every potential outcome, and then we avoid the necessary conversations completely. We pretend that if we just ignore the cracks, they'll go away. But unfortunately, they won't. As much as we wish them away, or sweep them under the rug, being honest in relationships is the adult thing to do. We've practiced being honest to ourselves so much throughout our time together so far; so let's channel those learnings into our relationships, too.

The first time that I practiced Speaking My Truth out loud in a manner that was mature and honest—with an intention of growing a relationship instead of hindering it—it honestly didn't work out the way I wished. By setting my boundaries and being vulnerable, I ended up crumbling a relationship that I thought would wither the quake. As I look back on this situation now though, there are no hard feelings. Because, when I finally spoke my truth in an adult way, it showed me that when our intentions are in the right place, being honest feels good no matter what the ultimate outcome is. Heck, it feels infinitely better than the passive-aggressiveness that happens when we avoid saying how we really feel. I'm sharing this experience with you now to demonstrate that even if a relationship ends when you stand up for your values, your world doesn't have to fall apart.

Honestly, I never expected to go through a friend break-up with Melanie. She was one of my first college roommates, and had become one of my closest friends well into my mid-twenties. Our relationship was built on honesty and depth—we talked about everything under the sun and seemed to just *get* each other. Even though we had moved cities and lived in different time zones, we always found the space to talk for hours on end.

So, when she did something seemingly innocuous on the surface that I thought was unfair and bothersome, I decided to approach her about it. In the past, I would have allowed this type of thing to fester out of fear, frustration, or simply immaturity. I didn't think it was my *job* to fix my friends, and quite frankly, it intimidated me. I didn't have the language or tools to manage conflict (and by the way—none of us do; resolving conflict in a healthy way isn't something we're born with as human beings).

But, as I entered my mid-twenties, I made a commitment to myself: if I was going to start living in my truth in all parts of my life, I had to start speaking it out loud, too. So, I took a breath and spent some time reflecting. I asked myself a few difficult questions: Why was this particular situation bothersome to me? Would it be helpful to acknowledge it, for both of us? What was my intention behind bringing this up? What would be an outcome that could help us both feel good? And, if the worst-case scenario did in fact happen, would I be okay with it?

Ultimately, after working through my answers to these questions I decided to speak up. Before reaching out to Melanie to talk about it, I got clear on what I wanted to say and wrote it down. I even practiced, almost as if I were going on a job interview, with Dupi on our couch. He pushed back and when he pretended to be the worst type of friend we could imagine, we laughed about it, because we could never imagine Melanie reacting in that way. I headed into our call feeling confident that I could be clear about my intention and see it as a space for both of us to grow as people.

But, guess what? At the very least, our conversation didn't turn out so well. It actually became close to the worst-case scenario that Dupi and I had laughed about days before. When I shared my thoughts with Melanie, she quickly became defensive and dismissive—and seemed to be caught completely off guard by my calmness. During our conversation, I shared that I didn't want or need anything from her perspective except knowing that she was aware of how her actions hurt my feelings. I wasn't expecting her to have a clear response in the moment, either. Heck, I knew I wouldn't if someone approached me about something I did that bothered them. Conflict resolution isn't in our human DNA, and we aren't exposed to a *good* version of it often. So, it makes it difficult for us to understand how to react when we're faced with it. Knowing that, my expectations for the conversation were really low to begin with. I really just walked into that conversation thinking that Melanie could hold space for my feelings, just like she had in so many other of our conversations.

Instead of doing any of those things (even days later after she had time to digest my thoughts), *she* ghosted *me*. I spent time trying to reach out and reconnect, even though I knew I had approached this situation in the most conscious way I could. I finally had to recognize that sometimes relationships need to grow apart, with the potential of growing back together at some point. And, this wasn't just my own assumption. Relationship experts across the board recommend that letting go of difficult relationships, when possible, is important for our personal health, stress, and longevity.

Since that conversation I've asked myself many times: would I have brought up my feelings with Melanie knowing what the outcome ultimately became? If I'm being honest, I would say yes (albeit hesitantly—losing friends is hard). Because, while I was saddened and surprised by losing my friend, this situation didn't feel the same as any other relationship shifts in the past, because I felt like I stood in my truth, I protected my boundaries, and I modeled the type of behavior I wanted to see. I said what I needed to say, without any baggage. I listened to my friend's frustrations and stressors. And, I held space for her to process these emotions, too, until I had to draw the line. And I found that when you are clear on your purpose, even if the situation goes to shit, you can still stand tall.

To be clear, not every (or rarely any) situation ends up this way when you stand in your truth. I've had so many difficult conversations since then, the large majority of which ended up strengthening that relationship instead of breaking it. But we do live in a world where Call Out Culture seems to be seeping through all of our interactions—whether it's with a stranger on Instagram or one of your uncles at the family dinner table. We've become so ready to root our heels into the ground based on our beliefs, and completely shut someone out of our lives based on their reaction to our "feedback." And while calling people out can be necessary in certain situations for sure, there's a baseline level of compassion, empathy, and understanding with which we can approach all of our relationships, whether that's a stranger or a best friend.

So, some of you might be wondering what exactly does it look like when you need to set those boundaries and have difficult conversations to preserve your relationships, and your own worth?

Since most of us People Pleasers struggle with the possibility of being disliked, we tend to avoid having the difficult conversations we need to have in the first place. What I've found to be extremely helpful (and what *Harvard Business Review* recommends) is a simple solution: approach these conversations with curiosity, instead of worry or fear. We can call someone in instead of calling them out. And, getting curious starts way before we begin the conversation.

Next time you need to set boundaries, or stay true to yourself with anyone in your metaphorical village—a co-worker, a best friend, a parent, a significant other, heck even a stranger—it helps to lead with curiosity and kindness if that's available to you. Difficult situations are difficult for a reason, so this isn't to say that you need to hide your real emotions, like anger, frustration, or fear. But, when you're thinking about approaching a difficult conversation you may give yourself some space before approaching it, and start by asking yourself some of the questions I outlined for myself before my conversation with Melanie, such as:

- Why is this situation bothersome to me?
- Is it helpful for me to say something in this moment?
- What would be the best case scenario after having this conversation for everyone involved?
-
-
-
-
-

Regardless of how the conversation goes, the only aspect you can control is your approach. Your intention. Your curiosity. As we grow older, it's our responsibility to uphold relationships, to make (and keep) new friends, and most importantly, to stand in our worth. So, as we continue to navigate this weird, confusing, and difficult part of growing up, keep in mind that while the relationship with yourself is the most important, the way you treat others is a clear reflection of what you believe you're worth, too.

— ELEVEN —

Throw Your Five-Year Plan Out the Window

How many times has the world not given a shit about all your hard work and thrown you a curveball anyway?

As human beings, we love to *feel* like we have control over every aspect of our lives. So, we create to-do lists and New Year's resolutions and five-year plans that very (very) specifically detail all the stuff we'll accomplish. We make sure our goals are SMART (Specific, Measurable, Attainable, Relevant, Time-based for all you folks who didn't get this drilled into your mind in school) while sprinkling in just enough elusiveness that they seem *almost* unachievable. We feel a sense of pride and productivity when we can dutifully cross one of those achievements off of our lists—whether that's picking up bananas at the grocery store or getting married by twenty-eight and a half.

But, in my twenty-odd years on this Earth, I've seen that the world often has other plans for us. Not to mention that *achieving* all of those goals, no matter how big or small or SMART or dream-like they are, often falls to the wayside when *life* stuff comes up instead. The world isn't taking your carefully laid out goals into account when it throws you a job offer in LA or a partner who lives in a distant country. Or better yet: a global pandemic as you're about to enter the Real World. When we're younger, we are both naïve and inexperienced enough to believe that we alone have the ultimate deciding factor on how our lives turn out. We believe that if we put just enough *hard work* and *dedication* into our life path, we'll end up going to the best college and marrying our best friend and checking off all of our perfect little boxes at the exact time we're meant to.

If this book hasn't shed just a tiny bit of light on how much stuff is influencing our lives beyond our control just yet, don't worry, we're about to get there. Our society is very much structured to make us believe that we alone have sole control over the life we create. I mean, look at the self-help industry. Businesses and books and diet trends and people's livelihoods have been built on this idea that if we just work a little harder, or follow a very specific (and not personalized at all) plan, we'll achieve said results. And, if that sounds crazy on this face of it, it's even more crazy that this industry alone is valued at ten billion dollars (and growing at over five percent each year) *just in the United States*. That's how much simply one country, one very self-obsessed country at that, spends on investing our hard-earned cash in motivational speakers, diet and weight-loss programs, books, and infomercials to supposedly rid our lives of problems and worry.

And while I'm not saying that our entire lives are a mess of random occurrences, we very much have control over our mindset and reaction to the randomness that is thrown on our path, we aren't necessarily taught how to think for ourselves. We aren't encouraged to color outside the lines, and more importantly, shown what to do when a big ol' paint splatter lands in the middle of your masterpiece. So, we're going to do something different than all those other self-help books you might read. Instead of tying together all of the work we've done over the course of this book so far into a nice, neat plan that you can follow to the tee so you can achieve the adulthood you've always dreamt of, we're going to learn how to roll with the punches, twists, and turns. We're going to craft a life map, one that leaves room for experimenting and testing and following random urges. Because, what's the fun in living a life that's so rigid, we can't even take a moment to breathe?

Motivation and surrendering can coexist

One of the hardest lessons I've ever had to learn—and trust, am still learning—is allowing myself to flow with the randomness of life. Giving myself permission to surrender control just a bit. Because, if you couldn't tell, my natural state is a bit neurotic. Growing up, achievement was my middle name. Even though it may not have been realistic, my parents made it seem like I could do anything I set my mind to. So, when I had my first not-according-to-plan moment at the age of seventeen, it felt like my entire world was shattered.

I'm sure many of you can relate to the nervousness that pervaded school hallways and AIM chatrooms around college acceptance time. Even if you claimed you didn't care about getting rejected from your top choice, you knew deep down that you *kind* of did. College letters were almost a form of social currency, even at my very mediocre public school where most kids ended up at a state college, anyway. Your peers would whisper and question which acceptance letters you received, moms would post their kid's successes on Facebook, even teachers would make marks on the chalkboard with the name of the school where you chose to commit the rest of your life.

Though there had been many times in my life before those letters started trickling in the mailbox when I had been rejected by something or someone (Mr. Dubin in the ninth-grade play, Ryan S. at the middle school dance among many, many others), college acceptances, or lack thereof, felt like a fatal blow of your own accord. It was the first time in my life where I felt like I had complete control over every aspect of this process—from late-night SAT preparation in my bedroom to sticking with Dance Team even though I hated it to rounds and rounds of essay writing. But you know, when those thin letters reached your doorstep you couldn't help but feel like a failure.

My personal dream was to attend Georgetown University. From the moment I stepped onto the campus during a family road trip to Washington D.C., I just *knew* it's where I belonged. Kids in popped Polo collars, ancient-looking libraries that creaked from the moment entered, hot lacrosse players—it seemed like a fairytale. I had always wished I had a "normal" name and strawberry blonde hair and parents who didn't have an accent, and this place just seemed so . . . American. I immediately translated this vision to a very specific goal in my diary: "Go to Georgetown undergrad and study pre-law; then go to Harvard Law School right afterwards." It just seemed *right* to me; after my doctor dreams had faded I immediately moved myself onto another very clear and outwardly "successful" path: law. So, Georgetown it would be.

Well, you all could guess how that story ended up. Waitlist letter after waitlist letter, my acceptance never came. I dragged my feet until the very last minute to send my acceptance into NYU (*It's so close to home, people are weird, I don't want to be in a city—I want to be on a campus in a city—don't you get it?*), hoping and praying that the Georgetown Admissions team somehow lost my letter in the mail. I'd be lying if I said I was excited to go to college that summer; I somehow just convinced myself that this would be an ink slip on my very carefully laid out life plan, transferring to Georgetown the following year and laughing about it at cocktail parties in my old age as that feisty grandma on vacation in the Cayman Islands (remember her?). I so badly wanted to be part of this fancy American world that I saw as the ultimate form of success, and Georgetown felt like it would be my golden ticket to get there. I resisted this random switch-up as much as I could, closing myself off to all the possibility that laid ahead of me.

So, when I got to NYU a few months later, I kept surprising myself with how much I *loved* it. I loved that I could just hop on a train to see my parents if I was feeling homesick (or more importantly that they could bring me homecooked meals without batting an eye). I was warming up to the hip and trendy people—I loved that my roommates were from Italy and Kansas and California, places that seemed so foreign to my Long Island bubble. I was obsessed with my professors who lived in Brooklyn and listened to This American Life and had toddlers named Lighting Bolt (I swear to God—I couldn't make this up if I tried). I was lit up by the energy of the city, that somehow, you could run into Big from *Sex and the City* on your walk to school *and* go to a sample sale in SoHo in between classes *and* intern at fancy magazines like *Allure* while taking a full course load. I was enamored and amazed and utterly confused at how *perfect* this very random, very unexpected life twist was turning out to be.

And so, little by little my Big Life Goals began to shift. *Maybe I would stay* was the first thought. Then, *maybe I'll study finance instead of law* was the second. I was opening up to the random and the unplanned—without losing my motivation and will to be the very best I could. I was slowly (very slowly) starting to balance surrendering control of the final outcome while still showing up as my best, most full self every single day. I was starting to witness that if I just allowed myself to see opportunities instead of failures, if I controlled my mindset rather than the stuff that kept showing up in front of me, life would not just be more fun, but more fruitful. It would unfold *exactly* how it was supposed to.

This nascent mindset shift began to trickle into how I approached everything in life. I still tried really hard, but opened myself up to all the opportunities I could instead of putting my blinders on. I talked to random people in coffee shops who ended up offering me jobs (it was tutoring, but in college cash is cash). And, as I got older I saw how magical this mindset shift could truly be.

During my first job at the bank-that-felt-like-hell, I knew I *had* to get out. I applied to job after job, to no avail. I felt like I had hit a brick wall but tried so freakin' hard I didn't know what more I could do. I had a clear plan, you see? But, the world wasn't doing exactly what I wanted it to. Out of sheer desperation, I started reaching out to anyone I had ever met that I thought was doing something interesting. Literally. It could have been people I ran into in the hallway during a college internship, or an acquaintance from high school. I was trying to figure out what I wanted to do next, so my only solution was to collect as much data as I could. I could only apply to so many jobs through LinkedIn a day.

So, one of those days, I met with an old college professor for coffee. I had reached out to her quite unsuspectingly but trusted my gut for a moment without questioning it. I didn't know her well, but I really enjoyed her classes and thought that she could have some interesting ideas for me to explore. Truth be told, I had zero expectations that I'd gain much from the conversation. So, you can imagine my utter shock when I learned that this seemingly random professor of mine was the president of a fancy philanthropic venture fund and offered me a job on the spot. She saw my sheer passion and interest in learning how to create impact in the world and asked if I wanted to join her team. The pay was incredible (they matched my salary at said-bank), the team was brilliant, the office was a beautiful loft in Tribeca, and it couldn't have been more perfect if I dreamt it up myself.

I had finally surrendered control a bit, and the world landed a big, fat, beautiful opportunity right in my lap.

I know these scenarios seem difficult to wrap your head around, because when you're caught in the middle of a dark time, when you're "going through it," it can be really hard to claw out of your mindset. It can feel like you just want to keep trying harder but you're not seeing any results. You know so clearly where you want to be, and it's Just. Not. Working. Everything feels like you're climbing up a mountain, and rocks keep crumbling down.

But, then there's one magical point when you kind of just surrender. You don't necessarily give up, but you let go of the reins a little bit. You shrug your shoulders and go to drinks with random old friends or let yourself simply just have fun for a moment. And then, the coolest, most interesting opportunities open up for you. They materialize with ease—so much ease that it almost seems impossible. You look around and wonder: "Is someone playing a trick on me?"

Finding this delicate balance can seem elusive, and quite honestly, there is no exact formula. I love the way that our friend, Michael Singer, describes his perspective on this in his book *The Surrender Experiment*: "My formula for success was very simple: Do whatever is put in front of you with all your heart and soul without regard for personal results. Do the work as though it were given to you by the universe itself—because it was."

It truly is that simple. As long as you hold your vision clear, act out of pure intention, and let go of the end results, life will truly unfold before you in a way that seems like pure magic.

So, screw those goals. We're living with intentions instead.

Five-Year Plans are so overrated

I know I'm going against conventional wisdom here, but we're not going to be setting goals together. None at all. But, what we are going to do is pull together all the stuff we've been talking about for the last few chapters: your life Right Now, your Ideal Day and North Star, your worries and fears, and your money mindsets and relationship matrix. We're going to put it all together so that you can truthfully see what your life looks like right now, what it's missing, and what might be holding you back from injecting more of that into it. We're going to get in touch with our feelings again (always) and map out what's really important to us so we don't lose sight of it through life's random ebbs and flows.

And then, we'll practice letting it all go.

Because, as you've learned from my own experiences, when we keep pushing against a wall that won't budge, when we have resistance around any aspect of our life and are acting from a place of achievement versus intention, nothing happens. We get frustrated and we end up giving up before we get to the good stuff. We become resentful and continue to tell ourselves the stories that prove our deep-rooted beliefs are real. And then, our Baby Brain looks at us and says, "See, I *told* you it wasn't possible."

This idea of reducing our resistance around an outcome and surrendering to the whims of the world can feel really unnatural at first. It goes against everything we've ever been taught. But, before we dive into building our Life Map built on this premise, let's get clear on what "surrendering" *is* and *is not*. Surrendering *is not* feeling a sense of failure, defeat, or frustration that we've somehow given up. It is *not* allowing ourselves to wallow in a state of despair or anger. It is *not* placing blame on ourselves because we should have controlled an outcome differently. Surrendering is, as the Queen of Dreams, Oprah, describes: "Not holding anything too tightly. Just wish for something, want it, let it come from the intention of real truth for you—and let it go."

Let's start to craft a life full of that intention, so when we do hit a roadblock we're able to tap into our real truth, as Oprah says, and simply let it go. This Life Map we're about to create will be a real embodiment of that. It's dynamic and everchanging and allows you to be open to all the randomness that might come before you, while also allowing you to have control over your values. To continue showing up as your best self no matter what. Because, that's all we could ask for in adulthood, right? To live a mindful, happy life that's entirely our *choice* rather than a constant negotiation.

So, we're going to bring together everything we've thought about into one place, so you can see those intentions ever-so-clearly. You can fill in your answers as reminders to each section, and then plot out where you are, and where you want to be, on the Life Map. Let's go:

LIFE MAP VISUAL

My North Star

This is my compass—it is the guiding light that will direct my life choices.

My Values

These three to five clear values are the intentions that I want to live by. They are the markers on my path that will tell me if I'm going in the right direction.

The Labels I'm Letting Go Of

Remember those labels we brainstormed in Chapter Three? Well we're going to remind our Baby Brains of what we're letting go of as we move forward.

My Nourishment

This list of needs, wants, and desires is derived from my Wealth Nourishment Pyramid, and other reflections we've done together. They are the checkpoints I will pass as I move through my journey.

How I Spend My Time

I spend my time in a lot of different ways, and I'm conscious about all of them. Some of it is at work, some is alone, some is partaking in fun hobbies.

My Village

These are the people that keep me connected, motivated, and happy. They support me and I spend my time, energy, and resources supporting them, too.

Where Are You Now + Where Are You Going

Use the map below to plot out where you are versus where you're going. How aligned are you with your actions versus your emotions? What does that look like in your Dream World?

LIFE MAP VISUAL

Now that you've made it through the tough stuff, the big-picture, reflective thinking, you're on your way. These lessons and exercises are meant to be practices that you build into your lifestyle; stuff that you continue to return to when you're confused or contemplating a decision-point. And, since they're such big shifts in thinking, they are anything *but* a quick fix. They won't just make your problems or worries disappear. That's on you, my friend—something you're 100 percent, completely, truly capable of. So, whenever you need to, as often as you need to, turn back to this section of the book and have a brainstorming session with your best friend—You.

Our next (and last!) set of work together is going to be around life changes you can make right now. They will be small rituals and practices that you can turn to when Adulthood gets too rough. And along with these big-picture practices, they will help you control your mindset so much that you'll feel like everything is in constant flow, that life is a continuous roll of choices. Let's go!

Part Four:

Let's Get It

Can you feel this energy? This is the start of something great.

-Khalid

— TWELVE —

Practice Being Kind to You, to Your Bank Account, To Strangers

When was the last time you said "thank you"?

Like, a serious thank you—not muttered under your breath at the Trader Joes checkout counter, or after you get a mediocre drink at the bar. I know what kind of "thanks" you're thinking of: the one you say with a side eye and half-smile, inching out of whatever place you're stuck in (line for the bathroom, running to catch a door someone is holding open for you even though you're still feet away). We're not talking about the simple cordial saying that has become so commonplace today. Rack your brain for a moment: when was the last time you said thank you and really, truly meant it? When was the last time you felt gratitude deep in your bones?

Nowadays, "gratitude" is a word that gets thrown around all too lightly. We hear it daily, scattered in yoga classes and *HuffPost* articles, on podcasts and lists of the stuff we "should" do in order to feel happier and healthier. So, we write in our gratitude journals for, like, three nights in a row and don't notice any changes.

We wonder what the heck we could be so *grateful* for in a world where schools and movie theaters aren't even safe. We search for some glimmer of hope in our very confusing, very stressful lives and can't seem to come up with anything that fits the bill.

For a long, *long* time I didn't get what everyone was talking about when they raved about this whole "gratitude" practice circa *The Happiness Project* heyday. For some reason, the idea of feeling grateful had a really high bar in my mind; it had to *mean* something. I didn't think it could just be a simple act of noticing like "feeling the sun on my face for a few moments" or a small, seemingly mediocre experience like "having an extra cookie that my roommate brought home for me." But, the issue really was deeper than my perception of gratitude. Actually, it was even more simple: I would never notice something to be grateful for even if it hit me in the face. I was constantly living in the past or the future, so I couldn't even wrap my head around the idea that the Right Now, the tiny, everyday moments in our lives, are the ones that make us feel insanely lucky to be alive.

The first time I ever heard someone speak about gratitude in a way that wasn't all fluffy puppies and trips to Costa Rica was during a really shitty scenario (isn't it always?): a major plane delay. It was my first leg of my travels to Australia and New Zealand back in 2014 and I was nervous. I mean, I was about to take the biggest, longest, scariest trip of my life to date. My mind was racing into the future (what if I forget something or don't make any friends or *completely hate it*?) and the past (I should have done more research or planned this better or had someone talk me out of this crazy idea altogether). The first leg of my trip was exciting and comforting, though: I was going to stop in Hawaii for a few days and stay with a friend I knew from college who grew up there. I did plan at least one thing right—I needed all the home-cooked meals I could get before heading off on this adventure.

I remember driving to the airport that morning with my dad, and of course, there was a major snowstorm. Of course! Some on the radio were calling it the biggest snowstorm of the decade. All I kept thinking as I looked out the window while we drove 5 miles per hour in standstill traffic was: "Wow, this is *just my freakin' luck*. Could this weather get any worse? This is not how I wanted my last few hours to be before the biggest trip of my entire life. Everything is going to be messed up now." While my dad, always the optimistic thinker, tried to calm me down, I couldn't seem to get out of my funk. Gratefulness was definitely not on my radar—not even a measly side-eyed thanks.

But, after saying goodbye to my parents and somehow making it through security with my very heavy Osprey backpack (think: the scene in *Wild* when Cheryl Strayed has to lay on the floor of her motel to get her pack on, except on the floor of an airport), I felt a little more confident, albeit sweaty and scared. It only took a few moments to make that false sense of security go away though—the moment that I saw that there were no TVs on the plane (what the heck, are we in 1980?) and heard an announcement that we'd be slightly delayed I turned into a nutcase. Any semblance of calm was gone.

Once we boarded, I took a deep breath, put my headphones on, and stared out the window to see pink ice getting thrown onto the wings of the plane. Fun. "*We're* never *getting out of here*," I thought. I crossed my arms and closed my eyes, hoping that I'd somehow fall asleep all the way to Hawaii. But, my short-lived dream was interrupted by a tap on my shoulder. I shot my eyes open, and pushed myself up in my seat, confused as to who the heck would be bothering me already. I slowly looked over to my right, and saw a very sweet-looking grandma with innocent eyes and tanned, leathery skin. My seatmate, we'll call her Shirley, looked at me with a giggle and a shrug, exclaiming, "At least we get to see a little bit of snow before we go!" I felt like I was going to vomit at her excitement; she was praising the very thing that I couldn't stop fuming over. *At least we see snow?* Who was this lady anyway?

Of course, I put on my very best fake smile and giggled with her, muttering sarcastically under my breath, "Yeah, well, hopefully it's only a little bit." I'm exaggerating but I'm sure, looking back on it now, Shirley could sense my closed-off and nervous energy though I couldn't see it myself. She began slowly, patiently asking me questions about my travels, my upbringing, and my future plans. It felt like Shirley was a literal ray of sunshine, melting my Ice Queen persona, one simple question at a time.

Shirley and I ended up talking for twelve hours (now that I think about it, everyone on that plane must have been really annoyed by us), and as I reflect on the people or interactions that have shaped my view of the world, she always rises to the top. Shirley was the pure embodiment of living a life full of gratitude, of presence, of kindness. During our conversation I learned that this crinkly, eighty-year-old woman with big, brown eyes was born and raised on a small island in Hawaii, in a tiny village. But, in her words, "[she] was so lucky to have been able to see the world outside of her little house." From the outside, Shirley's life wasn't necessarily one you'd inherently think is *lucky* by any means. From what I learned about her, she grew up quite poor, and her only daughter died at a young age, leaving Shirley to care for her granddaughter alone. But, nearly every word out of Shirley's mouth was laced with awareness of how special it was that she was flying on a plane, that she had food to eat, and that she was connecting with other human beings. It was amazing to watch as an innocent, not-so-kind bystander.

We often hear about gratitude and *living in the present moment* as stuff we can check off of our long to-do list. We try to incorporate these mindset shifts into our very busy, very stressful lives—only practicing them when we're on a yoga mat or relaxing on a very expensive beach chair. But, Shirley showed me, simply through her way of being, that practicing gratitude and simply saying thank you like you mean it can—and should—happen in the most mediocre of moments. Like, when you get an extra package of macadamia nut snacks from your flight attendant. Or when you simply describe the love you have for a person you care about to a complete stranger. You know, the simple stuff.

This chapter and the rest of our time together will be about all the simple stuff: the ways that we can start making our lives better, happier, healthier, and more joy-filled right *now*—not when your dream life finally comes into fruition, or you quit your job or find your forever person. Because, one of the most important aspects of living a life on purpose is taking action toward becoming the type of person you always wanted to be. It's balancing the ability to engage in deep reflection, to feel our feelings with *actually* doing something about it. It's recognizing that nothing will ever be perfect, so we can get started living the life we imagine for ourselves—no matter how weird it feels or bad we are at first.

So, let's get started.

Yes, in fact, we can become nicer over time

It's easy to think that gratefulness just isn't in your bones. Sometimes, we're taught that being a Debbie Downer is just *who we are*. We think that some people are born to be happy and optimistic, while others are anxious and negative. And while, yes, there are certain genetic factors that influence how we react to certain situations, there are actually scientifically-proven practices that we can engage in every single day that are known to shift the neurons in our brain to be happier. We all have the capacity to change. I mean, we already know how much of our Baby Brain controls our actions without us even realizing it. But, what if we flipped the switch? What if we began taking tiny, everyday actions to create new pathways in our brain that will help us become nicer to ourselves, our friends, strangers, and even our bank accounts?

There is a long-held understanding in most Eastern belief systems that what you practice grows stronger. In our science-focused world, we understand this concept as neuroplasticity—or that repeated actions and experiences shape our view of the world. By doing something again and again, whether it's taking the same commute each day, or getting frustrated when your train is one minute late, we restructure our brains to access this way of thinking more easily. Over time, these actions and beliefs become automatic; they truly become part of us as new pathways are formed in our brains. I think this piece of research is so cool, because over time if we pay attention to it, we can literally shift who we are just by becoming aware of the actions we take, the thoughts we think, and the way that we perceive the world.

At its core, this scientific research is at the essence of mindfulness, an age-old way of being that is most often practiced in Asian traditions. Mindfulness is simple; it happens when we become completely aware of the present moment. It's not just meditation, as some of us might think, although meditation is a tool that helps us get there. I love this definition by psychology professor and author, Shauna Shapiro, PhD: "Mindfulness has three elements—one, simply is paying attention. We spend over 47% of our lives *not* paying attention. Two, is *how* we pay attention; our values are like a compass guiding our path. And the final element is your attitude. Mindfulness is about paying attention with kindness, openness, and compassion."

Interestingly, in Asian languages the words "mind" and "heart" stem from the same root, so, Dr. Shapiro likens the word "mindfulness" to mean "heartfulness." How cool is that? This perspective shift for me, and I'm sure for many of you, is massive. For a long time, I thought that mindfulness just wasn't for me. It was too crunchy. Too weird. And heck, there was absolutely no way that I could sit still for five minutes, let alone twenty. I wrote this practice off as something that just wasn't my thing. But, over time when I reframed this seemingly intense commitment as simply living with *heartfulness*—approaching life fully, with intention, and a curious, compassionate mindset—how could you not want to take part?

At the core of this approach to life is really, truly recognizing the power of the moment we're in right now. Spiritual leaders and neuroscience experts alike all come back to the same message: when we allow ourselves to stop worrying about the future or freaking out about the past, we create more space in our life for living fully in the present moment. And living in the now allows us to release the fear or worry or stress that accompanies all those thoughts that circle around our Baby Brain 24/7. The coolest part, in my opinion, is that being fully present doesn't take much; there are no fancy tools or gratitude journals required. It's simply just becoming aware of you and your mind, your feelings, and your perspective. It starts with noticing.

Before we tap into some simple tools that can help us cultivate heartfulness and live in the now each day, let's begin to reframe how we perceive "the now." Because, time is a weird, confusing thing—as we already know from our vent session in Chapter One. Interestingly, the Ancient Greeks were onto this confusion, and came up with two different ways of describing time. In his book, *Essentialism*, Greg McKeown describes these concepts in modern terms: "The first [concept of time] is **Chronos**. The Ancient Greeks saw it as an elderly man, and his name literally connotes the ticking clock, the kind we measure (and race around trying to use efficiently). **Kairos** refers to the time that is opportune. It is experienced when we are fully in the moment, when we exist in the now."

That difference is powerful. In our modern world, we often only experience Chronos—as we run from meeting to workout class to dinner, tied to that very handy calendar we all know so well. But Kairos is powerful. It's the moment we get in the flow. It's when time feels like it stops. It's limitless. Pause for a moment and think: how often do you allow yourself to experience Kairos—or are you only living in a world dictated by that elderly man with the ticking clock?

Start saying thank-you right now

I'm going to challenge you to begin practicing heartfulness in this very moment. We're going to shift the hardwiring of our brains right now. I want you to close your eyes—or even just look up from this book for a moment, and think back to a time this week (today, even) when you got mad or frustrated. It could be at a co-worker who stole your comment in a meeting, or even yourself when you sent a weird text to a person you like. Who knows (who cares, really). It doesn't need to be a big thing.

Now, truly imagine yourself in that moment. Feel the anger and frustration. Experience whatever came up for you. Allow your Baby Brain to step aside for a second, and start to get curious. Approach your feelings with compassion and kindness. Simply, ask yourself: What made you react that way? What if you could practice being a little kinder next time? Slower to react? Let the curiosity about what's possible flow.

This tiny mindset shift is called a *Metta Meditation*, and it literally translates to "loving-kindness" meditation. See, meditation is easier than you think! In Buddhist tradition, this practice is at the core of *heartfulness* and allows us to take that ability to be kind, compassionate humans to the next level by sharing it with others. You could take this practice one step further and experiment with sending love or kindness (or basically anything but anger) toward that person. You could test the waters by sending those kind thoughts to yourself. You could do it while sitting in your car during rush hour traffic or on your way home from a late work meeting.

My favorite part about these practices is their accessibility. We don't need to be on that sandy beach or have everything perfect in our lives in order to start practicing them. In fact, it's much more impactful if you turn to these practices in moments of difficulty. It helps us create a foundation of safety, love, and happiness even when we feel like shit. It helps us truly get into The Now.

In this very moment, you might not understand the hype. Take what you wish from these practices. You might try this in a scheduled way, sitting on your couch and getting curious about something that frustrated you that day, three times a week. You might journal about it. You might wake up each morning, like Dr. Shapiro does, and greet yourself with a simple: "Good morning, I love you." Or you might think all of this is bogus, and completely unnecessary.

But, if you find yourself falling into the last category, I would challenge you to get curious about it. Approach your reactions with kindness, curiosity, and compassion. You'd be surprised at how radical this shift can be. It might even be, dare I say—*fun*.

— THIRTEEN —

Having Fun Is Underrated

When was the last time you did something just for *fun*?

For a long time, I thought that having fun meant I was lazy. That fun meant wasteful. That any time I prioritized fun over work, I wasn't doing my "best" and I probably wouldn't be taken seriously. So instead, I found myself continuously searching for it deep in my crowded Outlook calendars or an ongoing email chain with friends that's titled: "Can we reschedule?!?!" I tended to turn my weekends into a long stretch of work and emails and obligations. And, when I finally did free myself from the intensity of living in our modern world, I looked at my side hustle to occupy my time—those activities that were *supposed* to be hobbies, my so-called "fun" time, but became part of my livelihood instead.

There are many other words in our society that have much higher social currency than "fun" does—like, "busy" or "productive" or "efficient." And, more than that—we've somehow convinced ourselves that fun has no place in our life equation until much, much later. We've become obsessed with the hustle and believe that if we're having fun, we're missing out on success.

But, when you take a step back from the lifestyle we've created for ourselves—one devoid of joy and leisure—you quickly realize the major toll it takes on our overall well-being. Aidan Harper, the creator of the 4-Day Work Week Campaign, even goes as far to call this #hustleculture dehumanizing and toxic: "It creates the assumption that the only value we have as human beings is our productivity capability—our ability to work, rather than our humanity."

I would argue that this concept is even worse than simply just making work our entire lives. Because, us Millennials have some added complexities. When we do finally cut ourselves a slice of real, unplanned, no-strings-attached fun, we run through all the ways we can show others *just how much* fun we're actually having. So, we stage pictures or share updates with the click of a button. And then, we linger on the thoughts of what others *think* about our fun for much longer than our content lasts. It's almost like we've forgotten (or maybe, never learned) what it's like to do stuff simply for the heck of it.

But, this isn't just about having fun versus working hard. It's about how we view our time, and if we see ourselves as worthy of taking a break. It's if we're constantly living in Chronos, or allowing ourselves to flow in Kairos for a bit. Because, in our world today, one plagued with burnout, loneliness, and stress, we've collectively created a warped view of time. We have stacked our schedules, and then when we do genuinely have time for leisure, we spend hours scrolling through our phone leaving us feeling unfulfilled and drained. We think we don't have "time" for anything enjoyable—but truly, we've only been taught to equate our perception of ourselves and others with how productive we are.

Listen, I'm speaking from recent (and yes, scarring) experience. For nearly my entire life, I struggled with incorporating fun and joy into my life as often as I should (unless it was the type of "fun" that comes along with sitting at a basement or packed-out apartment party, which is really not so fun if you know what I mean). There have been many times when I've been so stuck on the work-gym-sleep hamster wheel that I didn't think I had time for it. I was too busy. I was too focused on getting ahead, on figuring out my *passion*, on building a life that *mattered*, so I left out one of the most important aspects: joy.

It honestly wasn't until I reached my mid-twenties and was jolted off my hamster wheel that I realized the importance of having simple, no-strings-attached fun. I was forced to reconsider how I spent my time, how I perceived my own "success" and confront the long-held beliefs I had about what I was *supposed* to be doing when I wasn't moving ahead to the Next Best Thing.

Growing up in the Tri-State area to immigrant parents in the early 1990s, hustle culture was instilled in me long before it was cool. You already know why. I was constantly shuffled from school to homework to extracurriculars, leaving little time for exploring or imagination. This training ground for success-sans-fun translated directly to my life as an adult, and I channeled that narrow-minded work ethic into every aspect of my being. I raised my hand for extra projects at work, even though I may have despised them. I started a blog and worked on this passion of mine until late evening hours on my couch. I signed up for running marathons and climbing mountains (literally), training for them in my "free" time. I just didn't feel whole if I wasn't being busy. Objectively, I thought that I was *having fun* the crazier my calendar looked. I still hung out with friends and made time for family. I still tried new restaurants and read new books. But there was always a major question lurking in the back of my mind: Am I doing enough?

Any time I had a spare moment, my thoughts would jump to the other stuff I could be doing, that I *should* be doing, trapping myself in the prison of my own mind. It would run through that never-ending to-do list. And, it didn't need to be work-related either. This always-on pressure ranged from super-overachiever mode (learn a new language) to small, daily tasks that felt like a requirement (workout classes scheduled weeks in advance). My hustle mode was ever-present and didn't seem like it was slowing down.

In fact, I didn't slow down until I was forced to. Until I moved to a place where leisure time was so integrated into the lifestyle, I was able to detox that East Coast Hustle right out of me. At the age of twenty-five, my then-boyfriend now-fiancé, Dupi, received a surprising too-good-to-be-true job offer in Silicon Valley. So, we packed up our tiny one-bedroom Brooklyn apartment and shipped ourselves across the country. Neither of us prepared ourselves for the personal changes we would experience in a city that *seemed* so much like our own from the outside. We left New York with the mindset that we would return soon, unscathed and maybe only changed by the tint of the California sun. But, living on the West Coast not only helped us chill out (literally); most importantly, it forced us to reassess how we spent our time and how we actually enjoyed it.

Because the culture around work was so different than anything we had ever known out in San Francisco, a few months into our move across the country, Dupi and I found ourselves amassing more and more free time than we'd ever seen. At first, we didn't know what to do with it. We went from having overscheduled calendars on top of constant email monitoring to getting rid of our Blackberry work phones *and* all the baggage that came with them. It felt like we were navigating unchartered territory, almost like we were bowling without the guardrails on. But soon the activities that brought us joy began to bubble up. Our work days ended earlier, so we made dinner together each night. Our weekends were filled less with answering emails and capturing our latest brunch excursions, so instead we took ourselves outside to explore. We started painting and learning how to make bread (Dupi, not me) and working on a never-ending puzzle that sat on our makeshift dining table. We felt so *lucky*, which of course, we were. But, we also began to question: why did it feel so special that we actually had time to do the stuff that made us feel alive? Isn't the whole point of being human, of life really, to enjoy the little stuff?

For some reason we think that our side-hustles are our hobbies

In our world today, this idea of "leisure time" is often conflated with many other ideas that aren't necessarily *free* time. Based on its Wikipedia definition (I honestly love this description), leisure is supposed to represent an experience that is completely, utterly free. I really resonate with the way it's described here: "leisure is time spent away from business, work, domestic chores, job hunting, educations, and necessary activities such as eating and sleeping." Because, so many of us view *leisure* as stuff that we're required to do in order to stay alive: Sleep. Eat. Connect with others. And then, the rest of our time is spent on work, side hustles, or getting ahead.

In her book, *Do Nothing: How to Break Away from Overworking, Overdoing and Underliving,* Celeste Headlee has uncovered some really interesting research and observations about the way our society has shifted over the past two-hundred years to prioritize *productivity* over *humanity*. Headlee believes that our obsession with work and efficiency could be traced back to the sixteenth century during the Protestant Reformation. She explains: "The concept of working your way to heaven meant that every idle hour was one in which you were not earning your spot with the divine . . . it was your *work* that made you a good person. And therefore, obviously, if you were not working all the time, you should feel guilty."

Headlee goes on to explain that the Industrial Revolution was another major jolt in our society's belief system. I bet you didn't learn about this part in high school though. Headlee goes on to emphasize, "I mean, it literally changed the way our species lived and worked—almost every aspect of it." Interestingly, we Americans aren't necessarily working more hours since the 1800s, but our national psyche *feels* like we are. We're overwhelmed, burnt out, and have *definitely* forgotten what hobbies look like. One sociologist even went as far to put it: "We're no longer keeping up with the Joneses—we're keeping up with the Kardashians."

With the advent of social media, our generation specifically struggles with understanding the difference between work, side hustles, and simply just having fun. According to a 2018 study, more than half of Millennials claim to have side hustles, which they now rely on for extra cash. While of course there's an inherent issue with the systems we're living in that Millennials need to seek out multiple different jobs just to pay their loans, we've monetized everything from our love of baking cupcakes to making videos of us singing weird songs. In her now viral article titled, "How Millennials Became the Burnout Generation," Anne Helen Peterson, a fellow Millennial, so eloquently described the tiring tightrope we're constantly balancing. She describes her over-packed, over-achiever lifestyle we all know so well as such: "It's not as if I was slacking in the rest of my life. I was publishing stories, writing two books, executing a move across the country, planning trips, paying my student loans, exercising on a regular basis." It's like she's describing the modern-day Gretchen Rubin. We've somehow become convinced that our lives need to be full of all that *stuff* in order to survive, to live, and even to thrive.

Now, it might seem frivolous to slot fun into our already over-scheduled days on the face of it. But, think about *joy* and *fun* as precursors to happiness. They're the insurance we have against "going through it" for too long and living a life filled with burnout, stress, and loneliness—our generation's tagline. Most importantly, joy and fun don't need to be these over-the-top experiences. We don't need to overachieve or overengineer their presence in our lives. I love the way that self-proclaimed expert on joy, Ingrid Fetell Lee, explains what joy actually *feels* like: "Unlike happiness, joy is momentary and small-scale: It comes from an intense feeling of positive emotion. It could be something that makes you laugh, or smile, for example, like watching a dog play or feeling the texture of sand pass through your fingers." Joy is small, but visceral. It's just as much about mindset as it is about the experience.

What do you like to do for fun?

It might seem like a simple question, but do you actually know the answer? When I asked the On Adulting community this question, the majority of them didn't have a clue. They conflated survival activities, like eating or exercise, with leisure. They brought up their side-hustles, like "writing a blog" that were laced with achievement. Or they said that they didn't have enough time for it, but admittedly spent hours on their couch, scrolling through their phone to "decompress" after work.

So, we're going to throw our previous training out the window and experiment with fun. Right now, we're going to create a Fun List, and then we're going to literally schedule them into our day. You know that I'm trying to break us away from this mindset of to-do lists and goal-setting, but in this context, we're going to get intentional about how we make time for *fun*. I know, I know—I feel like Miss Frizzle telling you to add a Magic School Bus ride to your agenda. But, while it might seem like it takes the joy away when we're creating schedules of fun, researchers have found that 30 percent of happiness actually comes from the *anticipation* of an event. So, let's create some space in our lives for a bit of joy in our lives, shall we?

In the space below, jot down some ideas of fun—pure, no-strings-attached fun—that you want to be more present in your life. There doesn't need to be a time stamp or an *Accomplish By* date either. It's a lifestyle shift, a perspective change. It's training yourself to think of something without a bigger purpose, without being the best, without turning this into the side hustle you always imagined. What small stuff can you do that will bring you more laughter, smiles, and moments of joy?

Your Fun List

Now that you have a clearer picture of some ideas of *pure fun*, can you think about the last time you actually did any of them? If you're going through this exercise and feel like your life looks bleak and boring, have no fear. There's always space to create more time for leisure activities (or what some of us might call "hobbies") into our every day—it's even as tiny as noticing a dog play at the park.

Typically, I don't recommend scheduling activities into our lives, but this calls for a different approach. You're going to make a commitment to me, your accountability buddy, and most importantly—You—to become what I call a *Leisurist*, or someone who consciously commits to living a fuller, more joy-filled life. You're going to pick two to three *pure fun* activities you brainstormed above and explain to me (and You) exactly when you're going to try your hand at them, what you need to get started, and how often you want to commit to this leisurely hobby. We're going to create some structure around our moments of Kairos; otherwise we'll allow that old man upstairs to control how we spend our time.

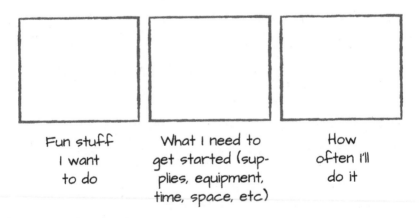

Fun stuff I want to do	What I need to get started (supplies, equipment, time, space, etc)	How often I'll do it

So, now that you've made your commitments to having some good, ol' fun, let's see how much fuller your life suddenly becomes. And, maybe you'll begin to notice how this insurance against burnout, stress, and loneliness is well worth your investment.

FOURTEEN

You Are Exactly Where You Need to Be

When was the last time you told yourself everything was going to be fine?

Well, if you haven't heard it in a while: You *are* going to be fine. Great, in fact. You are amazing and wonderful and exactly where you need to be. You're allowed to (and definitely should) slow down for a moment and take it all in. You've been able to get yourself *here*—a place where you're safe and thoughtful and have the rest of life in front of you. You are a capable, wonderful human being with the potential not just to change the world, but your entire view of it.

Us Millennials (and heck, anyone who felt called to pick up a book like this one) put a lot of pressure on ourselves to get it right. To succeed with flying colors. To check all the boxes and pass all the tests. Throughout our time together, we've come to understand why we humans in our modern world are like that—and that it's not *fully* our fault. We've seen the implications that everything from economic shifts to parenting styles to even the way our brains process negative information can impact the decisions we make throughout our lives. But, we've now been armed with tools, information, and a new perspective to shift our path. We've shown ourselves that yes, we can have fun while also creating meaning for ourselves and others. And, we can be grateful for it all—even when life might feel weird and confusing.

There's one magical aspect of living a life that's full of choice instead of negotiation that we haven't talked about yet: The freedom that comes with knowing every single thing is working out for you—and it always will. Now, I know that this idea of completely surrendering to the stuff that's showing up in your life *and expecting the best* sounds really difficult and unattainable. When I was "going through it" there was no way that I could keep my head above water every day, let alone trust that everything was moving in the right direction. By practicing the art of standing in your worth, letting go of your expected outcomes, and believing everything is working out for you, you are actually just shifting your perspective. It doesn't take anything fancy. You're literally just allowing that damn Baby Brain to simmer down and instead, let your deeper knowing take charge.

Remember when I told you about the first time I noticed voices in my head? Well, it was then that I realized there was a difference between my Baby Brain—her loud and repetitive tone—versus my Real Me, who spoke in a confident, kind, and calm voice. The Real Me was always sure that no matter what, I had myself to fall back on. No matter what, I could figure it out. No matter if I was stuck in the middle of nowhere in a dead-end job or heck without a job in my parents' basement or even in the negative spiral of thoughts in my head, I could get out. I could trust myself, The Real Me, to figure out what I needed next and act from a place of true connectedness. The Real Me always knew that everything would work out for me, no matter what. To me, this is the ultimate form of self-care: having a strong and consistent ability to trust that the future looks pretty damn bright.

We're going to practice together one last time accessing The Real You part of your brain, so that during times of toughness you can remember it. I often find that developing a set of mantras, or repeated phrases that I can use to help pull me out of my seemingly never-ending spiral of negative thoughts, ones that make me feel like my world is ending, is a deeply important practice in my daily self-care. You can think of it as a workout for your mind so that when you're stuck on a crowded, sweaty subway or a frustrating meeting (or worse), you're able to slow down those racing thoughts jumping around in your Baby Brain and trust in the possibilities that are flowing your way.

The concept of mantras, otherwise known as affirmations or repeated phrases, isn't something that simply gained popularity on Instagram or by being plastered on trendy t-shirts. It's an age-old practice that's derived from yogic, Hindu tradition and is deeply based on the belief of disciplining the mind. That's literally what man-tra means in Hindu: "to discipline the mind." So, after all of our time together, why not end off with a tactical, sustainable practice that's always available to us and can literally help us strengthen our mindset?

Before we get to writing out our short, everyday mantras, I want to get us in the headspace to do so. I'm going to give you the room to write yourself a love note. It might sound cheesy, I know. But, think of it as a long-form reminder that you can turn to during the times when you *go through it*. Now that you're armed with the tools, mindsets, and practices, you can put yourself in the position to imagine the future and remind yourself of all the good stuff that's to come.

Each year, I go through this exercise on my birthday. You can do it anytime, but I love treating this practice as something almost sacred. It's a real, live pump-up note that reminds me how freakin' far I've come—the stuff that we don't often think about when we're trudging through our everyday. It's quite different than a simple gratitude journal or list of all the stuff you're proud of. It's literally a letter to Me from Me as if I was an admirer from afar, soaking in the amazing stuff that's already happened, and yet to come.

I'm going to share an excerpt from the Love Note I wrote to myself on my twenty-third birthday. Looking back on it now, I could cry (well, every time I read it back, I do). Not out of sadness, but out of sheer love, truly, for that younger me. I'm in awe of how worldly and naïve and honest and kind she was. I am in love with her growing love for herself. I am so proud of her vulnerability and her sheer willingness to trust in her future.

Think of this note as a letter not just to Me, but also to *you*. Read it as if you were writing this to yourself. And then ask yourself: What will your Love Letter look like?

A Note to Me from Me:

Happy Twenty-Third Birthday circa Katina's Journal (2015)

I can't believe I'm twenty-three. Twenty-freakin-three. That's three years older than a twenty-year-old. Five years older than my eighteen-year-old self. I'm freaking out. I feel so old.

But, you know what?

I'm also twenty-three years young. I'm young and free and have my whole life ahead of me. I'm not yet jaded, but no longer naïve (well, sort of). I feel like I'm finally starting to hit my groove.

I'm also confused.

Last year, at this time I was refreshed and excited and oblivious about my future. I did cool shit, because I was not yet encumbered by the monotony of the everyday adult life. I was unaware of the fact that in a few short weeks, I would start my first real job and be starkly confronted by the questions: Who am I? What do I want out of this thing called life? What actually makes me happy?

Because, this year was really all about finding myself. I was pushing and pulling. I traveled and literally found my soulmate. I opened my eyes to other backgrounds and cultures. I saw beauty, and was challenged by new languages, people, religions, heat, lack of sleep, crowded subways.

I also started my first real job and settled into my first real apartment. I fell into a depression (I think) and thought that I could fix it by just forgetting about it. Hint: I couldn't. There were times I couldn't even take care of a plant, let alone myself. I was constantly pushing myself to do more, to be better. I ran a marathon. I tried to write a book. I worked a shit ton. I forced myself to think about my future. I took my first real "vacation" and somehow found myself again.

And, my relationships changed, too. I made new friends, and lost old ones. I met Dupi. I almost moved to London. I decided to follow my heart instead and stayed in New York. I chose my city and my person, even though I had no clue what to expect. I made plans and scrapped them, a million and a half times.

Most importantly though? I fell in love. I fell in love with myself, again and again. I also learned what it's like, what it's really like, to yearn and care and ***love*** *something bigger than myself.*

Even though I'm learning, I'm still confused. So, today—on my twenty-third birthday—I got my palm read.

I know it sounds stupid, but I ached for someone to tell me that life wouldn't be so confusing anymore. But, this woman took one look at me and instead, read my heart. She said that I needed to open up to life and look inside myself for what I need. I had to stop relying on the rules and let my guidance come from deep within. She told me exactly what I needed to hear.

But, I didn't need that lady to tell me that. I know, I ***know****, that everything will work out for me. I also know that I miss adventure. I miss doing cool shit on my own terms. I'm over Corporate America and being "curious" about stuff I don't care about and pretending to like people and things and days that I genuinely don't. I'm over "soliciting feedback" and "raising my hand" and telling "folks" about my life and interests and goals when I know they don't really care.*

So, I'm going to set some intentions about the year of twenty-three. I'm going to start bending the rules . . . for good. Here we go:

- *Stop being so nice (have a backbone, girl!)*
- *Listen better / actively / more*
- *Publish this journal into a book (if that means starting a blog, do it!)*
- *Be more balanced in my free time*
- *Sweat once a day*
- *Stop making excuses—take action where I can*
- *Explore exotic places and channel some adventure*
- *Find (and do) what you love*

So, Katina, go off and start doing. Have fun. Be passionate and thoughtful and excited. Be easygoing and critical and loving. Be ready for this next phase of your life—because I know it's going to be so freakin' amazing, I can't hardly wait.

Be you, forever and always. I love you.

And, happy birthday.

– *K*

Your turn, my humans:

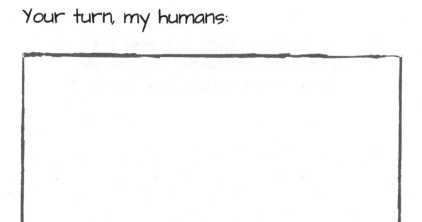

We're going to cut the sap and end our time together with real, actionable, and sustainable tools that we can use every single day to strengthen our mindset. In the space below, you're going to write yourself three mantras that you can turn to each day, maybe based on your Love Letter above. These mantras can be *so* simple. Honestly, the simpler they are the more powerful they will be. These clear sentences are meant to channel your highest, best version of yourself, so your Baby Brain can quiet the heck down. My favorite forms of mantras are basic reminders of who I am deep down, so I can begin to bring those values forward in my everyday life.

Here are a few examples of mantras I love and use personally in my own life. You might want to use mine for now and develop your own over time. There will also be a space for you to brainstorm a few consistent messages from your highest self, your Truest You, to say when you're in a time of need. Here are mine:

I am [fill in the blank with what feeling you want to channel—for example, calm, compassionate, kind, clear]

I am worthy of love. I am worthy of connectedness. I am worthy of everything that flows to me.

Everything is always working out for me.

Your turn:

So, now it's my turn to leave you with one last message. One last Love Note, so to speak. Because, our time together throughout this book has been nothing short of beautiful. It's been hard and weird and confusing at times, yes. But, it's also been deep and loving and kind. It's been reflective and grounding. It's been full of growth.

It's been, really, just like our journey into Adulthood.

And, if we can all take a step back to see both of these journeys—both during our time together and the process of growing up writ large—as beautiful, weird, confusing, and connected voyages towards knowing our true, real selves better, then well, that's all we can ask for.

So, know that just as that random fortune-teller I met on my twenty-third birthday reminded me: the answers are always within you. Stop looking outside of yourself, and tune in to your heart instead.

I love you, forever and always.

Epilogue

I like gettin' old.

-Patti Smith

No need to hurry. No need to sparkle. No need to be anybody but oneself.

-Virginia Woolf

Who Do You Want to Be When You Grow Up?

You may not have ever asked yourself this question, maybe not until right now. You've likely worked through the risk-return, logistical choices like I did for so long, weighing your percentages of possibility against your answer to the question. You, like me, were probably searching for the trophies at every turn. You answered based on what the "right" outcome was—what the adults in the room would respect.

But, we know how much words matter. They really matter. And, when we start paying attention to the little stuff—the words we use in daily conversation, the ideas that pop up in our head, the resistance that holds us back—we notice how much space opens up for change.

So, *who*—not what—do you want to be when you Grow Up?

I didn't always think in this manner, but I remember the moment when everything clicked for me. I was standing in line at Whole Foods on a normal weekday afternoon during a time in my life when I gleefully saw this trip to the supermarket as a form of upleveling from my twenty-five-cent banana runs years before. This time was not unlike my zombie excursion as a college student back then, but now I was watching my fellow grocery shoppers with curious abandonment instead of with fearful anticipation. I saw moms with baby spit-up on their sweatshirts and tech bros decked out in Patagonia gear scrolling through their phones to pass the time more quickly. Both groups were waiting for this errand to be over, just like everything else on their to-do list.

But, as I stood in that line with a shopping cart filled with groceries of my choosing instead of a sole, bruised banana, a fancy credit card and an Amazon Prime account to my name instead of twenty-five cents, I realized that a tremor of major shifts was beginning to ripple through me yet again. Because, as I looked at all that stuff, the stuff I collected over time, the stuff I thought was an important signal to *who* I was, I realized that none of it mattered, really.

What mattered was *who* I was deep down. What I cared about. What causes I fought for. What I practiced in my everyday life. What values I lived by, during the best of times and the worst. It mattered who I was, not what stuff I was defined by. And, as I observed all these people around me, those who were focused on collecting and showing others their trophies, I wasn't necessarily worried or stressed as my younger self had been years before. I was more reflective. Understanding. Aware. I also saw my fellow shoppers' own evolution and how difficult it was to see through all the stuff we were constantly collecting.

But I knew that this simpler way of living and thinking was possible—for all of us. I knew that tuning into my values deep down was the way that I truly wanted to be. I wanted to navigate adulthood mindfully, consciously, and happily. I wanted to act out of pure intention for me and continue to imagine a world that was kind, compassionate, and fair—one where the rules were always bending toward the better.

And so, as I waited patiently for my turn in line, I smiled at my fellow strangers. I knew that for many of them, this might have been the first real smile they saw all day. And, instead of feeling overwhelmed and stressed out by this impending Zombie Apocalypse before me, I was aware that by simply being myself, I could be their first ray of light.

By living according to *who* I wanted to be, I could show others the way, too.

I hope that's what this collection of words, stories, and ideas has done for you, my friends. I hope that it's been your first smile in recent days (or many) that's allowed you to look inside and see your light. To give you your power back, so you could continue passing it along to others. Because, what's the point of growing up if we can't all be in it together?

Love you all. Forever and always.

—Katina

Acknowledgments

This book is a compilation of experiences on this weird, confusing journey into adulthood—most of which didn't feel so great at the time. But, to all of them I am thankful.

I am especially thankful to my forever sidekick, story-listener, situation-analyzer, and best friend in the entire world: Dupi. He has been with me on this journey from almost the very beginning; together, we have evolved from very confused twenty-somethings to not-as-confused twenty-somethings. I couldn't be more grateful that this dreamy human stumbled into my life at the exact right time. Because of that, he's made the confusing parts of life a lot less lonely and the inspiring parts a lot more beautiful.

Of course, I am grateful for all the amazing humans I have in my life who have kept me sane, grounded, and happy: My mom and dad; my siblings (Nikki, Chris, and Peter); my best friends who have become (or already are) family—Anjelica, Jessica, Tess, Jasnir, and many others; and last but not least, the On Adulting community. Without this engaged, thoughtful, and vulnerable crew of people, this book wouldn't be in your hands today.

I am so honored and thankful for my Skyhorse Publishing family. When I was asked to write this book, I couldn't have been more surprised (I literally felt like Mrs. Maisel's dad when he's asked to work for Bell Labs in the show—trying to play it cool but jumping out of his skin with excitement). I can't wait to see what else we can put out into the world together.

And, last but not least—for all of you. For every single person who picked up this book. For every single human who is now equipped with the tools, foresight, and ability to make change. For you, I am grateful.

Resources

We know how much words have the ability to change the world. This list of books and resources are some of the words that have shifted *my* world view for the better. I hope that you take the chance to absorb their learnings, advice, and ideas for yourself (and maybe share them with someone who needs it!).

Creativity

Big Magic: Creative Living Beyond Fear by Elizabeth Gilbert

The Artist's Way: A Spiritual Path to Higher Creativity by Julia Cameron

Do Nothing: How to Break Away from Overworking, Overdoing, and Underliving by Celeste Headlee

The Runaway Species: How Human Creativity Remakes the World by David Eagleman and Anthony Brandt

Soul-Searching

The Four Agreements: A Practical Guide to Personal Freedom by Don Miguel Ruiz

The Untethered Soul: The Journey Beyond Yourself by Michael A. Singer

The Surrender Experiment: My Journey into Life's Perfection by Michael A. Singer

A New Earth: Awakening to Your Life's Purpose by Eckhardt Tolle

Career + Life Choices

The Crossroads of Should and Must: Find and Follow Your Passion by Elle Luna

You Are a Badass at Making Money: Master the Mindset of Wealth by Jen Sincero

Let My People Go Surfing: The Education of a Reluctant Business Man by Yvon Chouinard

The Blue Sweater: Bridging the Gap Between Rich and Poor in an Interconnected World by Jacqueline Novogratz

Promise of a Pencil: How an Ordinary Person Can Create Extraordinary Change by Adam Braun

Notes and Background Reading

Things Are Not Always What They Seem

Sifferlin, Alexandra. "Here's How Happy Americans Are Right Now." *Time*, July 26, 2017.

Clifton, Jim. "The World's Broken Workplace." *Gallup*. June 2017.

"The State of Creativity Study." Adobe. April 2012.

"Loneliness Index Study." Cigna. May 2018.

"Global Mobile Consumer Study." Deloitte. 2016.

Let Me Tell You A Secret

Page, Danielle. "How Imposter Syndrome is Holding You Back at Work." *NBC*. October 25, 2017.

Clance, Paul Rose, and Imes, Suzanne. "The Imposter Syndrome Phenomenon in High Achieving Women: Dynamics and Therapeutic Intervention." Georgia State University. Fall 1978.

It's Not (Fully) Your Fault

Kenny, Sarah, and Wang, Ming-Te. *Longitudinal Links Between Fathers' and Mothers' Harsh Verbal Discipline and Adolescents'*

Conduct Problems and Depressive Symptoms. Society for Research in Child Development. September 3, 2013.

Mlodinow, Leonard. *Subliminal: How Your Unconscious Mind Rules Your Behavior.* Vintage Books, 2012.

Eagleman, David. *Incognito: The Secret Lives of The Brain.* Pantheon, 2011.

Ruiz, Don Miguel. *The Four Agreements: A Practical Guide to Personal Freedom.* Amber-Allen, 1997.

Singer, Michael Alan. *The Untethered Soul: The Journey Beyond Yourself.* New Harbinger, 2007.

Trophies, Awards, and Lies, Oh My!

Gottlieb, Lori. "How to Land Your Kid in Therapy." *The Atlantic*, July/August 2011.

Doepke, Mattias, and Zilibotti, Fabrizio. *Love, Money and Parenting: How Economics Explains the Way We Raise Our Kids.* Princeton University Press, 2019.

Bialik, Kristen, and Fry, Richard. "Millennial Life: How Young Adulthood Today Compares With Prior Generations." *Pew Social Trends*, February 14, 2019.

"Finale." *Master of None.* Season 1, Episode 10, Netflix, November 6, 2015.

Mischel W., Ebbesen EB., Zeiss AR. *Cognitive and Attentional Mechanisms in Delay of Gratification.* Journal of Personality and Social Psychology, February 21, 1978.

Tsabary, Shefali, interviewee. "On Spirituality, Ego, And What to Do When Our Kids Are Unkind." *The Mindbodygreen Podcast*, Season 1, Episode 81, Mindbodygreen, 2019.

Stop Living in The Safe Lane

Matthews, Dylan. "23 Charts and Maps That Show the World Is Getting Much, Much Better." *Vox,* October 17, 2018.

Vaish, A., Grossmann, T., & Woodward, A. (2008). Not all emotions are created equal: The negativity bias in social-emotional development. *Psychological Bulletin,* 134(3), 383–403.

Tolentino, Jia. *Trick Mirror: Reflections of Self-Delusion.* Penguin Random House, 2019.

Preidt, Robert. "Depression Striking More Young People Than Ever." *WebMD*, May 11, 2018.

Binau, SG., Cooper, BA., Duffy, ME., Joiner, TE., Twenge, JM. (2019). Age, Period, and Cohort Trends in Mood Disorder Indicators and Suicide-Related Outcomes in a Nationally Representative Dataset, 2005-2017. *Journal of Abnormal Psychology.*

Soeiro, Loren. "Why Are Millennials So Anxious and Unhappy?" *Psychology Today,* July 2019.

Buettner, Dan. *The Blue Zones: Lessons for Living Longer from The People Who've Lived the Longest.* National Geographic Books, 2008.

Ruiz, Don Miguel. *The Four Agreements: A Practical Guide to Personal Freedom.* Amber-Allen, 1997.

Mlodinow, Leonard. *The Drunkard's Walk: How Randomness Rules Our Lives.* Vintage Books, 2009.

Ferriss, Tim. "Fear-Setting: The Most Valuable Exercise I Do Every Month." *Tim Ferriss Blog.* May 15, 2017.

It Starts with Telling the Truth

Inglis-Arkell, Esther. "Why Do We Smile and Laugh When We're Terrified?" *Gizmodo*, October 7, 2013.

Hendel, Hilary Jacobs. "Ignoring Your Emotions Is Bad for Your Health. Here's What to Do About It." *Time*. February 27, 2018.

Cameron, Julia. *The Artist's Way: A Spiritual Path to Higher Creativity*. TarcherPerigee, 1992.

You Won't Get in Trouble for Daydreaming Here

Brandt, Anthony, Eagleman, David. *The Runaway Species: How Human Creativity Remakes The World*. Catapult, 2018.

"The State of Creativity Study." Adobe, April 2012.

So, What Do You Really Want?

Williamson, Marianne. *Return to Love: Reflections on the Principles of a Course in Miracles*. Harper Collins, 1992.

Perel, Ester, interviewee. "The Relationship Episode: Sex, Love, Polyamory, Marriage and More (with Ester Perel)." *The Tim Ferriss Show*, Season 1, Episode 241, The Tim Ferriss Show, 2018.

Luna, Elle. *The Crossroads of Should and Must: Find and Follow Your Passion*. Workman Publishing, 2015.

Ekman, Paul. *Emotions Revealed: Recognizing Faces and Feelings to Improve Communication and Emotional Life*. Holt Paperbacks, 2007.

Murphy, Kate. "Outsmarting Our Primitive Responses to Fear." *New York Times*, October 26, 2017.

Ferriss, Tim. "Fear-Setting: The Most Valuable Exercise I Do Every Month." *Tim Ferriss Blog*. May 15, 2017.

Mo' Money, Mo' Problems

"National Postsecondary Student Aid Survey." National Center for Education Statistics, U.S. Department of Education, 2019.

Sincero, Jen. *You Are A Badass at Making Money: Master the Mindset of Wealth*. Viking, 2017.

Changing You Means Changing Relationships, Too

Goleman, Daniel. "The Group and The Self: New Focus on a Cultural Rift." *New York Times*, December 25, 1990, Section 1, Page 37.

"Millennials Are the Loneliest Generation." YouGov. YouGov Realtime, 2019.

Tiwari, Sarvada Chandra. (2013). Loneliness: A disease? *Indian Journal of Psychology*.

Seppala, Emma. *The Happiness Track: How to Apply the Science of Happiness to Accelerate Your Success*. HarperCollins, 2016.

Perel, Ester, interviewee. "Are We Asking Too Much of Our Spouses?" *The Ted Radio Hour*, Season 3, Episode 4, NPR, 2014.

Denworth, Lydia. *Friendship: the Evolution, Biology, and Extraordinary Power of Life's Fundamental Bond*. W. W. Norton & Company, 2020.

Manly, Dr. Carla Marie. *Aging Joyfully: A Woman's Guide to Optimal Health, Relationships, and Fulfillment for her 50s and Beyond*. Familius, 2019.

Garfinkle, Joel. "How to Have Difficult Conversations When You Don't Like Conflict." *Harvard Business Review*, May 24, 2017.

"Difficult Conversations: Discussion Guide." LeanIn.org and Fred Kofman, *Lean In*, 2013.

Throw Your Five-Year Plan Out the Window

Schwartz, Alexandra. "Improving Ourselves to Death." *The New Yorker*, January 8, 2018.

Singer, Michael Alan. *The Surrender Experiment: My Journey into Life's Perfection.* Harmony, 2015.

Winfrey, Oprah, interviewee. "Power, Perception & Soul Purpose." *Goop Podcast*, Season 1, Episode 1, Goop, 2018.

Practice Being Kind to You, To Your Bank Account, To Strangers

McKeown, Greg. *Essentialism: The Disciplined Pursuit of Less.* Currency, 2014.

Shaffer, Joyce. (2016). "Neuroplasticity and Clinical Practice: Building Brain Power for Health." *Frontiers in Psychology.*

Shapiro, Shauna PhD. *Good Morning, I Love You: Mindfulness and Self-Compassion Practices to Rewire Your Brain for Calm, Clarity and Joy.* Sounds True, 2020.

Having Fun Is Underrated

Griffith, Erin. "Why Are Young People Pretending to Love Work?" *The New York Times,* January 26, 2019.

Headlee, Celeste. *Do Nothing: How to Break from Overworking, Overdoing and Underliving.* Harmony, 2020.

"The Average Side-Hustler Earns Over $8K Annually." *Bankrate.* 2018.

Lee, Ingrid Fettel. *Joyful: The Surprising Power of Ordinary Things to Create Extraordinary Happiness.* Little Brown Spark, 2018.

Rubin, Gretchen. "Get More Bang for Your Happiness Buck: Revel in Anticipation." *Psychology Today*, February 2, 2011.

About the Author

Katina Mountanos is a renowned writer and creative entrepreneur who founded *On Adulting*, the viral blog and community to help her fellow Millennials navigate adulthood in a mindful and happy way. Her work has been featured in *Teen Vogue, Fast Company, Huff-Post, Mindbodygreen, Elite Daily, and* other publications.

Katina graduated from NYU's Stern School of Business in 2014 and began her career in data analytics at Goldman Sachs. She quickly realized her deep desire for social impact, helping to formalize and lead Goldman's environmental sustainability work, moving into philanthropic consulting soon after. Katina's early career has largely focused on bending the rules for good—most recently, she cofounded a mental well-being startup called Daydreamers to redefine how we all spend our "free" time.

Katina is currently pursuing her Master's in Clinical Psychology from Columbia University. She lives in Brooklyn—and around the world—with her fiancé, Dupi, and rescue pup, Wythe.

onadulting.com
@onadulting